MW00975127

PRAISE FOR *THE POWER OF PERSPECTIVE*

"Bruce Witt in *The Power of Perspective* helps every person to make a difference in this world by changing their viewpoint and aligning themselves with God's perspective. The principles will help you prioritize your life, be intentional about your decisions, pursue excellence, and live abundantly. Your journey be greatly enhanced in this life and throughout eternity."

Horst Schulze
Co-founder and former COO of Ritz-Carlton Hotel Company and Former CEO, Capella Hotel and Resorts

"My friend Bruce Witt understands the wisdom of cultivating an eternal perspective in our earthbound temporal arena. His new book on *The Power of Perspective* is a clear and concise guidebook to achieving skill in the art of living our pilgrim life with purpose and hope by treasuring the promises of the triune God."

Ken Boa
President, Reflections Ministries

"In *The Power of Perspective*, Bruce moves to the heart of the matter with practical simplicity and clarity. Having the right perspective will change your world. A thought-provoking and timely read that changed my life."

Francois Rauch
Global Operations Vice President, Harvesters Ministries

"*The Power of Perspective* is HUGE as Texas. I have known Bruce for over 45 years. This viewpoint, *if you practice it*, will allow God to take to you places you would have never dreamed of."

Stan Bower
Area Director Dallas-Fort Worth, Christian Business Men's Connection (CBMC)

"*The Power of Perspective* not only provides us with a roadmap for our journey, but it also provides us with an understanding of the things that will cause us to take disastrous detours and the attractions of life that are counterfeits, keeping us from the true destination. We need to read this book and reflect on our personal journey."

Bill Cousineau
Founder and CEO, Entrepreneur Development Box

Bruce Witt is 'A Man for All Seasons' (Robert Whittington) and *The Power of Perspective* helps to build the characteristics to navigate all of life's seasons and challenges."

Ian Ferguson
Dean of Southern Polytechnic College of Engineering and Engineering Technology, Kennesaw State University

"As someone who's been discipled by Bruce for over two decades, I've had a front row seat to experience his true wisdom, real grace, incredible generosity, and honest leadership. *The Power of Perspective* is a terrific book and like Bruce, refreshingly simple, but beyond wise. If you apply the principles in this book, you get to live your *best life* knowing Jesus is at the center! Great work Bruce!"

Trey Miller
President, Southern Andiron & Tool Co.

"Bruce Witt has been a great inspiration to me during very trying times, and his new book on *The Power of Perspective* has summarized many of the gold nuggets he has shared with me over the years. It is truly life-changing! Where the head goes, the body follows. Perception precedes action. Right action follows the right perspective. If you need a change of perspective, then this book is a must-read. A great book by a great author."

Thinus Botha
East Africa Director, Harvesters Ministries

THE
POWER OF
PERSPECTIVE

HOW YOU VIEW LIFE DRIVES HOW YOU DO LIFE

BRUCE R. WITT

THE POWER OF PERSPECTIVE

ISBN: 978-1-7328200-7-4

Published by Leadership Revolution Inc. Learn more at www.LeadershipRevolution.us

Copy Editing and Interior Layout: James Armstrong, UpWrite Publishing

Cover Design: Michael Sean Allen

Leadership Revolution, Inc.
Bruce Witt, President
4465 Nassau Way
Marietta, GA 30068
678-637-9890
Bruce@LeadershipRevolution.us
www.LeadershipRevolution.us

September 2022 Printing

CONTENTS

THE POWER OF PERSPECTIVE

Chapter 1

THE BIG IDEA

"Perspective is everything when you are experiencing the challenges of life."
—Joni Eareckson Tada,
a quadriplegic from a diving accident

Recently I was picking up my car at the auto repair shop, and I asked the store manager, "How is business going?" He said, "It's OK—but our biggest challenge is that we can't find enough labor to fill our available positions. But in light of what other parts of the world have to contend with, we're doing pretty well. Villagers in my home country have to walk five or six miles from their houses to the river to get muddy water to live on for the day. And then they have to walk the same distance back home carrying their heavy loads. They do this every day. I can walk into the next room and get clean water, instantly, for no cost, and have as much as I want. So, for me, life is good—it is a matter of perspective."

How we think about live life and the circumstances in which we find ourselves is greatly influenced by our perspective. Are we seeing things as we want them to be or as they really are? Do we see life from a positive viewpoint or do we believe we are victims and that life isn't fair? Do we think we deserve more? Do we see circumstances being controlled by the hand of God, or is it all up to us to make things happen?

What if I told you that it was possible to gain a fresh perspective that will help reshape your view of life and the things that go on every day? The Lord wants us to enjoy life because He made us and this world. If we can look at our lives and the circumstances from God's perspective, we will possess a new hope, a thankfulness, and a joy that will satisfy us and encourage others. So, as we discuss "perspective," it's *this* kind of perspective—God's perspective—that we are referencing.

What are you facing? What challenges and difficulties are you going through that are coloring your perspective? The premise of this book is that when we gain a new perspective about our life and circumstances, it will transform us and shape our attitudes and actions, preparing us for an abundant life.

Our perspective can give us the power to rise above the challenges of life's circumstances rather than being buried by them. Perspective can change everything we encounter—things that make us feel good or things that are very challenging. A proper perspective of life is vital to having intimacy with the Lord, clarity of purpose, and possessing a fruitful life in eternity.

We all need perspective, but too often we limit ourselves in our vision: our processing, our choosing, and our actions fall short. We tell ourselves things that are not true or are only partially true, and we end up sidetracked or in the ditch. Perspective forces us to think and consider our choices, from there we decide and take steps of faith on a journey that is to be lived and embraced in order to consistently live above the circumstances of everyday life.

THE BIG IDEA: How we view life drives how we do life.

Let's briefly unpack this idea. The backdrop or context of the power of perspective is recognizing that life is a journey of ups and downs, joys and losses, and growth and setbacks. Seeing life as a journey helps us understand that life is a process. We don't go alone, it is not a competition, each step is important, and there is a good destination.

There are three components to The Big Idea: viewpoint (how we view life), influence (drives), and action (how we do life). How we view ourselves, our world, other people, and the circumstances around us are a framework that guides and motivates our actions.

The viewpoint is made up of spiritual, emotional, personal, relational, and practical aspects, which can be thought of as lenses or filters. Each of these lenses brings information and understanding for us to process and take action. Through them we will discover keys of The Power of Perspective, which include seeing, thinking, surrendering, choosing, acting, and living. Our viewpoint depends on where we are at a particular moment in time. A good example of different perspectives of an event can be found in these quotes, *"As to the difference between a recession and a depression, Beck* [Teamsters Union President Dave Beck (1894-1993)] *said: 'I define a recession as when your neighbor loses his job, but a depression is when you lose your own'"* (*The Daily News*, New York, 15 Feb. 1954).

"I have already learned the difference between a Recession, a Depression, and a Panic. A Recession is where you tighten your belt; a Depression is when you haven't any belt to tighten, and a Panic is when you have lost your pants."

The influence is the internal motivator and guide by which we process the information collected from our viewpoint. It includes recognizing that we all are on a path of many possibilities. In navigating the path of possibilities, we will encounter several crossroads that will channel us toward taking action.

The actions we take in our journey all carry an eternal mindset in a temporal world. This dual view influences us in a specific point of our journey now, and it also carries us toward a future destination. For example, it is in embracing an eternal life both now and forever that gives us joy and abundance.

The Lord's desire is to be completely engaged in our walk, helping us to grow and flourish. He should be central to our viewpoint, influence, and actions so that we fully live life with the power of His perspective.

This "Life Journey" is not for the casual observer or the faint of heart. We are all called to make a difference and take on the challenges that come our way. God has great things in store for each of us who will grow, follow, and persevere. Life is a journey with good and challenging situations. Thankfully, we are not called to go it alone, we need one another for strength, encouragement, and comfort. Our journey's destination is eternal life and an eternal home, something we all long for, something this life can't offer.

> *"If we find ourselves with a desire that nothing in this world can satisfy, the most probable explanation is that we were made for another world."*
>
> —C. S. Lewis

Maps provide direction and help us plan our next steps. One can't go from the start to the end in one step. The Power of Perspective is a map or a route to follow so we know where we are going. It builds our confidence and allows us to enjoy the stops along the way. Knowing where you are in life allows you to grow and take steps in faith. The Power of Perspective enables you to see how far you have come and what lies ahead.

The journey we will take to discover perspective and experience its transforming power has six parts:

1. **Understanding Your Current Reality and Challenges.**
2. **Embracing the Benefits of Perspective**
3. **Gaining the Power of Perspective**
4. **Navigating the Possibility Path**
5. **Playing the Long Game in the Moment**
6. **Go Change the World**

As we embark on this journey let me encourage you with a reminder to be open to what God wants to do in and through you.

> *Once upon a time, there was an old farmer who had worked his crops for many years. One day his horse ran away. Upon hearing the news, his neighbors came to visit. "Such bad luck," they said sympathetically.*
>
> *"Perhaps," the farmer replied.*
>
> *The next morning the horse returned, bringing with it three other wild horses. "What great luck!" the neighbors exclaimed.*

> *"Perhaps,"* replied the old man.
>
> *The following day, his son tried to ride one of the untamed horses, was thrown, and broke his leg. The neighbors again came to offer their sympathy on his misfortune.*
>
> *"Perhaps,"* answered the farmer.
>
> *The day after, military officials came to the village to draft young men into the army. Seeing that the son's leg was broken, they passed him by. The neighbors congratulated the farmer on how well things had turned out.*
>
> *"Perhaps,"* said the farmer.
>
> —An Ancient Parable

David G. Gallan explains: "It's not that the farmer is unengaged in life. It's not that he is unable to be happy or sad. But he has a greater perspective. He sees the bigger picture. He knows that he can't stop things from happening, but he can control how he reacts to them. And it's often not the experience that matters as what you do with that experience." We've all had experiences where the curse turns into a blessing, rejection turns into redirection, and the unanswered prayer is the best thing that could've happened to us.

Life is indeed like a box of chocolates—you never know what you're going to get. Yet the farmer in the story above isn't delusional or apathetic, but calm and composed through life's ups and downs. And there's a subtle expectation that fortune will follow his misfortune. It's important to have foundational beliefs that keep you composed and allow you to appreciate and celebrate the good and to process trials, knowing they soon shall pass.

A True Story of the Power of Perspective – Annie Johnson Flint

Annie Johnson was born in 1866, and following the death of her mother, her father took Annie and her sister to board with the widow of an old army comrade who had been killed in the Civil War. They were eventually adopted by the Flints, whose name thereafter they bore.

5

But, as her adoptive mother was failing in health, and already had had one slight stroke, Annie felt that she was really needed at home, so she started teaching the primary class in the same school that she had attended as a girl. According to her contract with the normal school, she taught for three years, though early in the second-year arthritis began to show itself. She tried several doctors in turn, but it steadily grew worse until it became difficult for her to walk at all, and she had a hard time finishing out the third year. After that, she was obliged to give up her work, and there followed three years of increasing helplessness.

The death of both her adopted parents within a few months of each other left the two girls alone again. There was little money in the bank and the twice-orphaned children had come to a real "Red Sea Place" in their lives.

Picture if you can the hopelessness of Annie's position when she finally received the verdict of the doctors of the Clifton Springs Sanitarium, that henceforth she would be a helpless invalid. Her own parents had been taken from her in childhood, and her foster parents both passed away. Her one sister was very frail and struggling to meet her own situation bravely. Annie was in a condition where she was compelled to be dependent upon the care of others.

Annie became thoroughly convinced that God intended to glorify Himself through her, in her weak, earthen vessel, and like Paul she had three times and more prayed that this might be taken from her. There came to her with real assurance the promise which said, *"My grace is sufficient for thee: for my strength is made perfect in weakness."* She reached the place where she could also say with Paul, *"Most gladly, therefore, will I rather glory in my infirmities that the power of Christ may rest upon me"* (2 Corinthians 12:9).

For more than forty years there was scarcely a day when she did not suffer pain. Her joints had become rigid, although she was able to turn her head, and in great pain write a few lines on paper. But long before these years of helplessness, she had received her one great affirmation from God which settled all her doubts. The following poem she wrote was upon the words, *"For all the promises of God in him are yea, and in him Amen..."* (2 Corinthians 1:20).

He Giveth More Grace

He giveth more grace when the burdens grow greater,
He sendeth more strength when the labors increase;
To added affliction He addeth His mercy;
To multiplied trials, His multiplied peace.

When we have exhausted our store of endurance,
When our strength has failed ere the day is half done,
When we reach the end of our hoarded resources,
Our Father's full giving is only begun.

Fear not that thy need shall exceed His provision,
Our God ever yearns His resources to share;
Lean hard on the arm everlasting, availing;
The Father both thee and thy load will upbear.

His love has no limit; His grace has no measure.
His pow'r has no boundary known unto men;
For out of His infinite riches in Jesus,
He giveth, and giveth, and giveth again!

THE BIG IDEA

Chapter 2

UNDERSTANDING YOUR CURRENT REALITY AND CHALLENGES

"To find where you are going, you must know where you are."
—John Steinbeck

Here's a definition of perspective: *the state of one's ideas, the facts known in relation to the outside world. Seeing all of the relevant data in a meaningful relationship. A mental viewpoint that sees and understands both the inside view and outside facts and brings them together in a meaningful way.*

In life you need perspective. You can't see everything—you are bound by space and time. Perspective begins with understanding where you are and being aware of what is going on around you.

The world has lost its true sense of reality as it is being manipulated by money, the media, power, and evil influences. The lack of perspective is rooted in a self-focused, self-serving world that only grows worse when there is a lack of true wisdom. With the lack of perspective and wisdom, we are blind, distorted, selfish, deceived, short-sighted, material obsessed, and dull. This leads to failure, pain, emptiness, hurt, anger, despair, and destruction.

Perspective with wisdom is one of the greatest needs of our time for us to navigate the challenges and trials of this world. It is also the best way to have a positive impact on our lives, our world, and our future.

Many have lost their way and live in a world that has lost a true sense of perspective. The world's view of life is temporal and distorted by an obsession with self and the importance of self. If the world has gone off the rails and is destined for the ditch and despair, we are too, unless we gain perspective and wisdom.

So how do you find perspective when the world has lost its way? Here are six steps to gain clarity of where you are.

1. **Stop – Cease Striving**
2. **Know Yourself**
3. **Take stock**
4. **Ask Questions**
5. **Seek Truth**
6. **Affirm Hope**

Stop – Cease Striving

We lived in a crazy busy world. The pace of life and the push of technology have increased our activity to the point of frenzy. When we are so busy, we have a hard time knowing not only where we are but where we're going. So, we must stop doing and just "be". We need to slow down. Psalms 46:10 says, *"Cease striving and know that I am God."* Another version says, *"Let go, relax and know that I am God."*

So, when we stop our activity, we can begin to rest and gain strength. This also allows us time to reflect on what is going on around us. We are not caught up in the frenetic pace and the vortex of the world forces.

What does "stopping" look like? It may mean just starting the day with quiet time. It might mean going for a walk or simply resting. Take a break—it might be 10 minutes or it might be an hour. Maybe you take the day off. Whatever measure it takes for you to "stop" will be challenging, because in your mind you have a "to-do list" that's longer than your arm and it feels like you can't stop or you will be farther behind. But this discipline of stopping and ceasing from striving is the first step to understand our reality.

When we stop, we must also show up—to be present in the moment—and not be distracted. Jim Elliott said, *"Wherever you are, be all there."* This means being settled and ready to listen or understand. Our attention must be fully on the person in front of us or the situation at hand.

Stopping also entails being at rest. True rest is found in trusting in Christ and His control; we let go of the outcomes and know in our hearts the Lord is at work. Only when we are yielded can we rest, and only in our rest can God work through us. This is known as "abiding" or "being at home with." In John 15:5, Jesus says, *"I am the vine and you are the branches he will buy it's me and I and him he bears much fruit apart from me you can do nothing."*

Know Yourself

> *"I do believe that knowing where we are, has a lot to do with our knowing who we are."*
>
> —Ralph Ellison

In order to know oneself, one must look at the personal, the practical, and the spiritual. Personal includes how we are wired, our personality, our likes, talents, desires, and needs. These are all internal things that we need to be aware of because they make up who we are. Included in the personal are our life experiences from the past with its good and its trauma, as well as our present situations. Additionally, it includes our aspirations, the vision of our future, and our desires to help give us an understanding of who we are. The practical is simply awareness of our current circumstances: where we live, work, and what is going on in our personal world.

The spiritual understanding of who we are is much more profound. It begins with an understanding that we're both forgiven and are "new creations in Christ." We have a new identity and a new spirit which affect our mind, emotion, and will. We'll cover this more in depth in a later chapter.

Take Stock

Be aware and be a student of the world around you. We live in a world of great challenges, political vitriol and divisions, and wars and conflicts worldwide. It is not all doom and gloom, but we do see good and evil in a very profound way.

We also must understand that the Bible says in the future there will be difficult days ahead, and so we must not be naive or only see the positive. We need a large dose of reality. The challenge in today's culture is that the media is very biased and will manipulate the story to serve their agenda.

Be continually aware of the forces we are up against every day and even every moment: the world, the flesh, and the devil. We are at war spiritually, and thus we need to be conscious of this reality to be well prepared.

Ask Questions

Learn to ask questions. In asking questions, we gain clarity and understanding at a deeper level. Do not be content to just take things on the surface or blindly accept what people say. Be curious, ask what is going on. Seek to understand the story behind the story. Ask why? What? How? Seek to know what people are feeling and what you are feeling. As we gain this clarity of understanding, we are in a much better place to move forward.

Seek Truth

We need to seek the truth of any situation. What are the facts? What is going on? We also need to seek truth from God's Word and the Spirit of Christ. It is in knowing the truth that we understand, and we also have a sense of direction, peace, and freedom.

Affirm Hope

The final action is to affirm our hope. Hope is foundational to who we are as well as our actions, our attitudes, and our walk of faith. Our hope is found in Jesus Christ and in the Bible. Hope is not found in the things that are temporal or the things that are pleasing in this world. These are not necessarily good or bad, yet they do not define our true hope. True hope is anchored in eternity, not in the temporal. So, as we have hope in

Christ, then we have a perspective that helps us at the moment and helps us to go forward.

A Final Note

The perspective of the current reality redeems the chaos by making the moment meaningful and the eternal rewarding. As we take hold of our current reality, we begin to tap into the power of perspective. Our current reality does not define or dictate our future. As Winston Churchill said, *"Success is never final and failure is never fatal."* The future has many possibilities, and as we are clued into current reality, we can begin well.

This poem by Rudyard Kipling connects the ideas of being aware of our surroundings and who we are. This is a sign of maturity.

If: A Father's Advice to His Son

If you can keep your head when all about you
Are losing theirs and blaming it on you,
If you can trust yourself when all men doubt you,
But make allowance for their doubting too;

If you can wait and not be tired by waiting,
Or being lied about, don't deal in lies,
Or being hated, don't give way to hating,
And yet don't look too good, nor talk too wise

If you can dream—and not make dreams your master;
If you can think—and not make thoughts your aim;
If you can meet with Triumph and Disaster
And treat those two impostors just the same;

If you can bear to hear the truth you've spoken
Twisted by knaves to make a trap for fools,
Or watch the things you gave your life to, broken,
And stoop and build 'em up with worn-out tools

If you can make one heap of all your winnings
And risk it on one turn of pitch-and-toss,
And lose, and start again at your beginnings
And never breathe a word about your loss;

If you can force your heart and nerve and sinew
To serve your turn long after they are gone,
And so hold on when there is nothing in you
Except the will which says to them: 'Hold on!'

If you can talk with crowds and keep your virtue,
Or walk with Kings—nor lose the common touch,
If neither foes nor loving friends can hurt you,
If all men count with you, but none too much;

If you can fill the unforgiving minute
With sixty seconds' worth of distance run,
Yours is the Earth and everything that's in it,
And—which is more—you'll be a Man, my son!

Chapter 3

EMBRACING THE BENEFITS OF PERSPECTIVE

"Although no one can go back and make a brand-new start,
anyone can start from now and make a brand-new ending."
—Carl Bard

Knowing where you're going and understanding its importance is one of the greatest motivators we need. We will look at the why of perspective, the benefits it brings to us when we embrace it, and the foundation of our perspective.

Why Perspective?

It is important to consider "why" perspective is so critical to obtain and live out. Here are ten reasons why we need to work on gaining a perspective on life and our subsequent actions. These speak for themselves.

1. **Knowing the Lord and His love will change your view of life. You will enjoy eternal life now and forever.**
2. **Attitude will determine the outcome. Your perspective will affect everything around you—positively or negatively. Our words and beliefs often will govern the result.**
3. **You can react or respond to challenges. Hope will sustain and deliver you in the trials. Doubt and fear will destroy you.**
4. **Very few people see life from God's viewpoint. Over 90% of the world lacks a biblical worldview.**
5. **Without perspective, the results can be disastrous. We make little progress if blinded by limitations or negative views.**

6. Perspective can open doors to impact and change the world.
7. God's perspective will keep you in His will. Perspective drives purpose, frames your priorities, and directs your practice.
8. We choose based on what we see and believe. As we think, so we become. Most live to meet their perceived needs.
9. There are always consequences to every decision—good or bad. We decide based on our perspectives.
10. Everyone has a perspective, some are more biblical and accurate, while others are more self-focused and deceived.

Take some time to reflect on these ten statements. As you do, make note of which ones you fully believe in and which ones you may be more skeptical of. This understanding of "why" will help solidify your journey in finding perspective.

The Benefits

God's perspective, when lived out, has many blessings and is a means of great gain now and forever. We will examine the value and benefits of perspective in five arenas.

1. Rises above the Chaos.
2. Sees a Bigger Picture.
3. Gives Focus.
4. Builds Stronger Relationships.
5. Impacts Our Eternity.

Rises above the Chaos

When we have a proper perspective, it helps us at the moment not to be persuaded by the storms and the challenges, but it gives us the means to rise above the chaos. We look at things from this higher perspective, and that helps us to be able to help others. This proper perspective allows us to bring hope to the downcast, our presence to those who are lonely, and comfort to the hurting. So, when we have this view of life, we can then give our lives away in service to others.

Sees a Bigger Picture

A key benefit of perspective is that it allows us to see unlimited opportunities. Our choices are not defined by good or bad or some limited thinking. This is especially true when our perspective is grounded in and founded on God's view. God wants the best for us, and He is going to work through us and give us unlimited opportunities to grow and carry on His mission.

Gives Focus

A godly perspective will also allow us to have greater focus. We will know the right priorities, and we can pursue them in the right order. This then yields better solutions and better outcomes both for ourselves and for the world around us.

Builds Stronger Relationships

When I embrace a proper perspective I also then value people in a greater way. I value people because God values people and that opens doors for relationships. Perspective is critical to having good relationships because we see people from God's perspective. And in these relationships, we also grow and benefit, because we gain wisdom from other people, insight, encouragement, and strength. A key aspect of being connected to other people brings this sense of a "collective IQ," combining the wisdom of one another. We don't have to be the smartest person in the room, because together we are much better.

Impacts our Eternity

A final benefit of perspective is that not only are my actions producing more fruit in this world, they are producing treasures in heaven. How I live my life in the moment will impact the quality of my eternity. Matthew 6:19-21 says, "*Do not layup yourself treasures on earth where moth and rust destroy thieves break in steal, but lay up yourself treasures in heaven were neither moth nor rust destroy nor thieves break in and steal, for where your treasure is your heart will be also.*"

We are destined for victory! With victory comes hope. A life of hope will help us and others alike. The victory is for today, for the eternal impact of reaching others, and a picture of heavenly rewards. The victory is marked by contentment, joy, and fruit of the Spirit. Taking hold of and exercising the power of perspective will help us be grounded so that we can live fully in this world, yet not be of it or sucked into it.

> *"I'm just thankful for everything, all the blessings in my life. I think that's the best way to start your day and finish your day. It keeps everything in perspective."*
>
> —Tim Tebow

A Solid Foundation

God Himself is the only solid foundation for seeking, understanding, and living with perspective.

1. God is in full control and not unaware or uncaring. We are not in control of life.
2. God is fully able to do any and all things He wills according to His eternal purposes.
3. God invites us into His purpose and plans. He is not all that interested in my plans.
4. God is relational, and He calls everyone into a personal love relationship with Him.
5. God has paid an infinite price for us and desires a relationship with us.
6. The fear of God is the beginning of wisdom and knowledge.
7. If we ask, God will give us wisdom in order to process perspective.
8. Life without the Lord is meaningless. Life with Him is eternal and purposeful.

Our Part

Perspective is founded on God's character, yet we must play a part. The following serves to set our thinking right as we dig into gaining the right perspective in the next chapter.

1. We play a part in the process and will be held accountable.
2. We are fully loved, secure, and valued. We can do nothing for God to love us more or less.
3. We are to live in the moment with a knowing and longing for our true home.
4. We have been given everything we need for life and godliness.
5. We are blessed and have unfathomable riches.
6. We are not defined by circumstances, although they can shape us and move us in a certain direction.
7. We pursue perspective because only with it can we navigate the meaning of life and our role in it.
8. We must be very careful not to listen to the lies of the enemy or the lies we tell ourselves.
9. We can live in peace and contentment when we have a godly viewpoint.
10. We are called to give our lives away in serving others.
11. Apart from Christ we are nothing and can do nothing.

Chapter 4

GAINING THE POWER OF PERSPECTIVE

"The journey of a thousand miles begins with one step."
—Lao Tzu

"If you don't know where you are going, you'll end up some-place else."
—Yogi Berra

We have defined our starting point of perspective and put forward our motivation for the journey. We are now ready to take the first steps. If we change our views, it will change our lives, and we will discover tools that will give us the ability to change the world. We will look at how to gain this power perspective in three different ways in this chapter: Wisdom, Life under the Sun, and an Overview of the six key actions.

Wisdom and "The Fear of the Lord"

The power of perspective is rooted in wisdom and growing that wisdom and its application within the context of the world, our culture, relationships, and enduring difficulties.

Fearing the Lord is a healthy balance of glorifying the Lord and humility. We find much of what the Bible says about fearing the Lord in the books of Psalms, Proverbs, and Ecclesiastes. Solomon builds on fearing God with the practical application of obedience. This is the conclusion of life under the sun and over the sun. In Ecclesiastes 12:13, he says, *"The end of the matter; all has been heard. Fear God and keep his commandments, for this is the whole duty of man."*

In discussing the fear of the Lord we will look at what it is, what are the benefits and blessings of fearing the Lord, how it enhances our relationship with God, and why we should fear the Lord for who He is and what He can do. We will let God's Word speak for itself on each of these topics and make some final conclusions.

- **To fear the Lord – being filled with Awe/Reverence. This is the reason why most people don't seek the Lord.**

> *"Let all the earth fear the Lord; let all the inhabitants of the world stand in awe of him!"* (Psalm 33:8).
>
> *"The fear of the Lord is to hate evil; Pride and arrogance and the evil way and the perverted mouth, I hate"* (Proverbs 8:13).
>
> *"Since we have these promises, beloved, let us cleanse ourselves from every defilement of body and spirit, bringing holiness to completion in the fear of God"* (2 Corinthians 7:1).
>
> *"There is none righteous, not even one; There is none who understands, There is none who seeks for God..."There is no fear of God before their eyes"* (Romans 3:11-18).

All people are called to fear the Lord through worship, praise, and thanksgiving. Most do not, and it leads to pride, arrogance, and hatred.

- **Benefits and Blessing of fearing the Lord**

> *"The fear of the Lord is the beginning of knowledge; fools despise wisdom and instruction"* (Proverbs 1:7).
>
> *"The fear of the Lord is the beginning of wisdom; all those who practice it have a good understanding. His praise endures forever!"* (Psalm 111:10).

"And he said to man, 'Behold, the fear of the Lord, that is wisdom, and to turn away from evil is understanding'" (Job 28:28).

"The fear of the Lord leads to life, and whoever has it rests satisfied; he will not be visited by harm" (Proverbs 19:23).

"The fear of the Lord prolongs life, but the years of the wicked will be short" (Proverbs 10:27).

"The fear of the Lord is the beginning of wisdom, and the knowledge of the Holy One is insight" (Proverbs 9:10).

"The fear of the Lord is an instruction in wisdom, and humility comes before honor" (Proverbs 15:33).

"Be not wise in your own eyes; fear the Lord, and turn away from evil" (Proverbs 3:7).

"The fear of the Lord is hatred of evil. Pride and arrogance and the way of evil and perverted speech I hate" (Proverbs 8:13).

"By steadfast love and faithfulness iniquity is atoned for, and by the fear of the Lord, one turns away from evil" (Proverbs 16:60).

"The fear of the Lord is a fountain of life, that one may turn away from the snares of death" (Proverbs 14:27).

"The reward for humility and fear of the Lord is riches and honor and life" (Proverbs 22:4).

"In the fear of the Lord one has strong confidence, and his children will have a refuge" (Proverbs 14:26).

"Praise the Lord! Blessed is the man who fears the Lord, who greatly delights in his commandments!" (Psalm 112:1).

"Behold, thus shall the man be blessed who fears the Lord" (Psalm 128:4).

"Charm is deceitful, and beauty is vain, but a woman who fears the Lord is to be praised" (Proverbs 31:30).

"Oh, fear the Lord, you his saints, for those who fear him have no lack!" (Psalm 34:9).

"And his mercy is for those who fear him from generation to generation" (Luke 1:50).

Fearing the Lord...

1. Adds strength to life.
2. Teaches a person wisdom.
3. Wisdom begins with it.
4. Enables a person to avoid evil.
5. Brings wealth, honor, and life.

- **Fearing the Lord enhances our Relationship with God. To those who fear God...**

"The intimacy of Lord is for those who fear him, and he makes known to them his covenant" (Psalm 25:14).

"Behold, the eye of the Lord is on those who fear him, on those who hope in his steadfast love" (Psalm 33:18).

"As a father shows compassion to his children, so the Lord shows compassion to those who fear him" (Psalm 103:13).

"His delight is not in the strength of the horse, nor his pleasure in the legs of a man, but the Lord takes pleasure in those who fear him, in those who hope in his steadfast love" (Psalm 147:10-11).

> *"But the steadfast love of the Lord is from everlasting to everlasting on those who fear him, and his righteousness to children's children"* (Psalm 103:17).

Fearing the Lord is rooted in having an intimate relationship with Him. And with this intimate relationship, we enjoy God's blessing and enter into His love for us.

- **Fearing the Lord for who He is and what He can do**

> *"And do not fear those who kill the body but cannot kill the soul. Rather fear the Lord who can destroy both soul and body in hell"* (Matthew 10:28).

Where does fearing the Lord come from?

Fearing God comes from an understanding of who God is and His ultimate nature. He is omnipotent, omniscient, and omnipresent. This defines both His character and His love. It also helps us understand that He is in full control, has our best interests at heart, and is continually pursuing us.

When we fully grasp God's unconditional love and that He desires to work in and through us, our response is that of both humility and praising Him at the same time. A right perspective truly understands Christ's forgiveness, His new life in us, and how He's growing and changing us into His image over time. This helps us overcome our emotions and fear as well as gives us a sense of worthiness and significance. This gives us an ultimate perspective about life because this is how God chose to make it.

Fearing God comes from knowing who we are in light of who the Lord is. We are not to think too highly of ourselves, relying on our strengths and talents and forgetting the work of the Lord in and around us. We need humility, which comes from knowing the Lord in His glory. Likewise, we are not to think of ourselves as worthless and of no value. The Father paid the price of Christ on the cross for each of us; thus, while we were unworthy, we are of infinite value.

Life under the Sun

As we are discussing the fear of the Lord, we note that many of the verses that talk about this come from Solomon. A unique perspective that Solomon had as he wrote both Proverbs and Ecclesiastes was the idea that life under the sun and life with God were two separate things. The following chart this helps us frame these two ideas and gives us further insight into developing a godly perspective.

Life under the Sun	Essence	God's View – Christ Life	Conclusion – Life above the Sun
Life Is Unmanageable.	Life is not fair. Bad people get ahead. Good people suffer. Our culture is headed over the cliff.	The Lord knows all, sees all, and is over all. He is Omnipotent, Omniscient, and Omnipresent.	**God is in control and on the throne.** Our broken lives are changed when embedded in His story.
People Are Unreliable.	We fail and will fall. We sin. We forget and let people down.	God's love is unconditional and unlimited. Relationships are made whole in Him.	**God is faithful and can be trusted.** He is our foundation and rock. He is at the heart of our relationsºhips.
Evil Is Undeniable.	Spiritual warfare is real. The enemy is working to stop Christ and hurt people. Evil is unvarnished in our culture and politics.	God wins the battle. The enemy will be defeated. Greater is He who is in us.	**The Lord is victorious.** He leads us in triumph, giving us courage.
Problems Can Be Unsurmountable.	We live in a fallen world. There is hurt, loss, and pain.	The Lord will see us through the problems. They can grow us. There is light in the darkness.	**God has our best interests at heart.** He knows what is best for us.

Aloneness Is Inconsolable.	Not good for us to be alone. Being alone increases the sense of loss and fear.	We are never alone.	**He lives in us, and we are in Him.** We are with Him always. Christ in us is our hope.
Future Is Unpredictable.	Life is uncertain. Fear and the unknown exist. Economics are fluid.	The Lord stands outside of time and knows all. He is the source of wisdom. Heaven is real.	**The Lord is eternal, and we are with Him.** We have eternity in our hearts.
Death Is Unavoidable.	Life is short and fleeting. We all die. The question is: Do any of us truly live?	Death has lost its sting.	**Death is the path to life.** Dying brings much fruit.

Six Keys Gaining the Power of Perspective

In the next six sub-chapters, we will unpack these six keys to gaining the power of perspective. This is at the heart of the action necessary to grow and make changes in our life.

1. **See Clearly – Look Beyond What You See.**
2. **Think Soundly – Wisdom Requires Reflection.**
3. **Surrender Fully – Fit to Quit.**
4. **Decide Boldly – You and Your Impact Are the Product of Your Choices.**
5. **Act Intentionally – Put Your Boat in the Water and Start Paddling.**
6. **Live Abundantly – Don't Waste Your Life.**

These six actions take wisdom and discipline. Consider this: in **seeing** we see dimly at best and all that glitters is not gold; in **thinking** we become what we think about, and no one ever has had a totally pure thought life; in **surrender** we come to the end of our human resources; in **deciding** feelings are not good signposts. **Activity** is not necessarily productivity, and **living** is more than growing old and surviving. We all need a fresh perspective of the Lord, of ourselves, our world, and how we walk through life. It will change us and impact the world.

Our prayer: "What we see not—show us; What we know not—teach us; What we have not—give us; What we are not—make us; Where we live not—guide us."

So, as we launch, consider these verses. *"Show me your ways, O LORD, teach me your paths; guide me in your truth and teach me, for you are God my Savior, and my hope is in you all day long"* (Psalm 25:4-5). We are challenged to ask the Lord to show us, teach us, guide us, and cause us to realize our hope is in Him.

Chapter 4 (a)

SEE CLEARLY

"Look Beyond"

"It's not what you look at that matters; it's what you see."
—Henry David Thoreau

Have you ever gone through a difficult experience and after some time you looked back and saw a bigger picture? Time can change our viewpoint. What we initially perceive to be terrible, transforms into something good. I have experienced this a number of times in my life.

Some years ago, I had a position of significant influence running the field staff of a large service organization. The president of the organization became upset that people were not buying into his vision and that, somehow, was my fault. The truth was that the vision was much more about external performance; it was self-focused and was primarily about appearing successful rather than truly serving and helping people.

I was pushed out and made the scapegoat. It was extremely painful and hurtful, not to mention very costly financially. The circumstances were very difficult at the time; I could not see any good coming from it. Some months later, I started an organization to develop leaders using a different foundation than the typical skill-based process. Over time we have had the opportunity to serve thousands of leaders who are literally influencing millions of lives.

This would have never happened in my previous role and company. Looking back, I see the Lord had to take me through a hard and dark valley to prepare and position me for multiplied impact and a greater future. I thank the Lord every day for His grace and the pain of that change.

Keep Your Eyes on the Prize

We must realize we live in a spiritual world, and we need to have our eyes open to the reality around us. We must distinguish the big picture from the activity. Only when we see clearly can we accurately understand our world, and then process the situation making wise decisions. Let's look at how Jesus modeled this and then consider how we see life from four different angles.

1. **See the Lord.**
2. **See Reality.**
3. **See with New Lenses.**
4. **See the Eternal.**

The Model of Christ

Jesus looked up to the Father for provision. Jesus modeled prayer and reliance upon the Father for supply in His time of need. *"And He took the five loaves and the two fish and **looking up** toward heaven, He blessed the food and broke the loaves and He gave them to the disciples again and again to set before them; and He divided the two fish among them all"* (Mark 6:41 NAS).

Jesus looked to the Father for blessing. At the very end of Jesus' life, He looks to the Father for both blessing and affirmation (glorify the Son). *"Jesus spoke these things; and raising His eyes to heaven, He said, "Father, the hour has come; glorify Your Son, so that the Son may glorify You"* John 17:1). If Jesus looked to the Father for both provision and blessing, this becomes a lesson for us to learn and practice. *"While we look not at the things which are seen, but at the things which are not seen; for the things which are seen are temporal, but the things which are not seen are eternal"* (2 Corinthians 4:18).

Observations:
- To see clearly is the first step in harnessing the power of perspective; otherwise we will be blind, deceived, or limited.
- We must cultivate seeing with an eternal hope to properly know the true value of things and how to treat them properly.

- Wisdom clarifies the meaning (why) and reality of our seeing, and these are founded only in Jesus Christ.
- Seeing the Lord from His viewpoint totally changes how we see the reality of life and its circumstances.
- We live and see things in a world that is temporal, full of inequity, and often a mystery.
- Becoming a steward will radically change our view of things and our handling of them. We transfer ownership.

> *"For in hope we have been saved, but hope that is seen is not hope; for who hopes for what he already sees? But if we hope for what we do not see, with perseverance we wait eagerly for it"* (Romans 8:24-25).

See God. *Look up.*

Gaining a new frame of reference from new vantage points helps us look at life and circumstances differently. What is your viewpoint? The view from the mountain is better than trying to see from the weeds. We are often called to look to the Lord.

> *"Look to the Lord and His strength; seek His face always. Remember the wonders He has done, His miracles, and the judgments He pronounced"* (Psalm 105:4-5).
>
> *"Lift up your eyes and look to the heavens: Who created all these? He who brings out the starry host one by one and calls forth each of them by name. Because of His great power and mighty strength, not one of them is missing"* (Isaiah 40:26).

Here are five different vantage points from which to look.

- *See from God's viewpoint.* Look down from above. We always see more when we look down and see from the ground level. Close your eyes and consider how is God looking at your situation.

- *See God at work around us.* Look around and join Him. When we see God working, we know we are in the place we need to be. One way to know God is working is to observe that people are seeking Him and asking questions about Him.
- *See Jesus.* Fix your eyes on Jesus. Look to and for Christ, author and perfecter of the faith. This takes discipline and a healthy prayer life, yet when we see Him, we are comforted and encouraged.
- *See Jesus in others.* Look at the good in others and how they may be serving others. This draws us closer to one another and to Him.
- *See spiritually with faith.* Look spiritually. Move beyond human eyes. Faith is the key to seeing with new eyes. Build up your faith.

We see by observing the character and nature of God. God stands outside of time and space. He is in control and has our best interests at heart. This gives us assurance and confidence. Our view of God defines who we are, thus for Christians, having a proper view of God is vitally important. Everything that we do in life is meant to revolve around God and give Him glory; we are His creations. *"And he is before all things, and in him, all things hold together"* (Colossians 1:17). *"Great is our Lord, and abundant in power; his understanding is beyond measure"* (Psalm 147:5).

- God Is Infinite – He Is Self-Existing, Without Origin
- God Is Immutable – He Never Changes
- God Is Self-Sufficient – He Has No Needs
- God is Omnipotent – He Is All-Powerful
- God Is Omniscient – He Is All-Knowing
- God Is Omnipresent – He Is Always Everywhere
- God Is Wise – He Is Full of Perfect, Unchanging Wisdom

See Reality. *Seeing from ground level.*

Having put on eyes of faith we also must taking stock of what is actually happening. Life is full of the good and the pain. We need to acknowledge what is real and accept it. We can fool ourselves or deceive ourselves.

> *"How can you say to your brother, 'Brother, let me take out the speck that is in your eye,' when you yourself do not see the log that is in your own eye? You hypocrite, first take the log out of your own eye, and then you will see clearly to take out the speck that is in your brother's eye"* (Luke 6:42).

- *Accepting reality.* See yourself rightly and then see others as the Lord sees them.
- *Encountering pain and loss – what is our response?* Begin with thanking the Lord for who He is and that He is on the throne. He is in perfect control.
- *Recognize that circumstances don't define us.* Embrace that as bad as things seem in the moment, the Lord can walk us through challenges to grow us and shape us for a better future.
- *Don't play the blame game.* Take inventory of yourself and make sure you are in a good place. Do not judge others; seek to help them.
- *Learn the life's lessons, good and bad, from others.* We don't have to learn everything personally. Study how others grow.
- *The ground level is dark with traps and snares.* Recognize that for the moment the enemy is seeking to kill, steal, and destroy.

See with New Lenses. *Seeing clearly.*

What kind of glasses are you wearing? We all see through a set of glasses or lenses that can color or distort the proper view of life. Paul on the road to Damascus was struck down and blinded. He cried out and, through the ministry of Ananias, came into the presence of the Lord who took the scales off of his eyes in order to see. We all need the Lord's presence to see rightly.

> *"For now we see in a mirror dimly, but then face to face; now I know in part, but then I will know fully, just as I also have been fully known"* (1 Corinthians 13:12).

- *See with open and clear eyes.* You can't see when your eyes are closed, blinded, or scaled over. We all have blind spots. We need others to help us see what we cannot.
- *Christ is the Light of the world.* When things are dark, we can't see well. Lean into Christ, who can shed light on any situation. This will change how we view things.
- *We all see through a set of glasses.* Our past experiences frame how we see things. Be aware of how you tend to see life.
- *Attitude colors how we see things.* See below.
- *Pain shapes perspective.* See below.
- *Expectations need to be from the Lord.* What we expect and desire can frame how we see things. Make sure your expectations are rooted in Christ.

Attitude colors how we see things. We have a choice about our attitude. Attitude is a way of thinking or having a perspective that is then reflected in a person's behavior. Attitude is one of the most important factors in helping you through life's ups and downs. Whatever perspective you may hold will invariably have an effect on your performance.

- Attitudes can affect our outcomes. They will help us determine the difference between having meaning or misery, in reaching a destiny or being in despair. It is the difference between success and significance.
- They help us turn tragedy into triumph. With a proper attitude, we can overcome pain, suffering, and trials.
- They help us move beyond self-centeredness, self-gratification, and pleasure seeking.

Pain shapes perspective. We are molded by suffering and can shape how we see things. In the pain and hurt, we need empathy and care. We don't need logic to try and fix or explain the situation. The pain can and should produce humility and a ministry flowing from us.

See the Eternal. *We live in a spiritual world.*

A great reward awaits us. If we are not careful we will be destined for the ditch without perspective. See from eternity. Wait on the Lord. Eternity becomes the foundation for a vision of our lives. Vision is more than seeing.

The final aspect of seeing is understanding how to see with or from eternity and an eternal perspective. Our lives are indeed short, so we must live with the future in view, especially in light of the challenges of our day. *"Not abandoning our own meeting together, as is the habit of some people, but encouraging one another; and all the more as you see the day drawing near"* (Hebrews 10:25). Are you looking for the Lord's return and how does that affect your living?

- *Following the Lord has a price.* It will require sacrifice and, at times, hardship.
- *Not following the Lord has a bigger price.* The price paid in the moment and in eternity can be large.
- *Every action and inaction have a consequence.* Our every thought, motive, and action will be judged.
- *The Lord is coming back.* Keep looking for the Lord's return; this keeps us from making earth our home.
- *Choose eternal reward over temporal gain.* Temporal gain may be pleasurable, yet the eternal reward has an infinite return.
- *Let it play itself out.* Don't try to correct everything in the moment. Don't be judge and jury. Let the Lord play His part.

> *"We don't yet see things clearly. We're squinting in a fog, peering through a mist. But it won't be long before the weather clears and the sun shines bright! We'll see it all then, see it all as clearly as God sees us, knowing him directly just as he knows us!"* (1 Corinthians 13:12 MSG).

> *"For now we see in a mirror dimly, but then face to face; now I know in part, but then I will know fully, just as I also have been fully known"* (1 Corinthians 13:12).

Questions

1. Why is seeing the Lord and seeing from His viewpoint so important?
2. What is the biggest thing blocking, blinding, or distorting your ability to see from God's viewpoint?
3. How is seeing life from an eternal standpoint so critical in our world today?

OBSERVATIONS: *We can see and still be blind. Deception starts with the eyes. All that glitters is not gold. Be careful not to react quickly to what we think we see. Look twice, study the details. Ask the Lord to show you.*

Application

1. Pray to the Lord to open your eyes to see how He sees.
2. Slow down to observe.
3. Overcome the world, the flesh, and the devil. Not doing so results in blindness and seeing dimly.
4. Look with eyes of faith in order to recognize the Lord, His ways, and His works.
5. Look into the future. What will the impact of your life be in 200 years?
6. Consider the eternal value of the things you do and focus on them. Note what and how much is focused on the eternal.
7. Put on the mindset of a steward, and give up ownership. Clarify your earning, spending, saving, and giving. Increase giving.

A prayer for the eyes of your heart: *"That the God of our Lord Jesus Christ, the Father of glory, may give you a spirit of wisdom and of revelation in the knowledge of Him. I pray that the eyes of your heart may be enlightened, so that you will know what is the hope of His calling, what are the riches of the glory of His inheritance in the saints, and what is the boundless greatness of His power toward us who believe"* (Ephesians 1:17-19).

> *"I believe in Christianity as I believe that the sun has risen, not only because I see it, but because by it I see everything else."*
>
> —C. S. Lewis
>
> *"The only thing worse than being blind is having sight but no vision."*
>
> —Helen Keller

SEE CLEARLY

Chapter 4 (b)

THINK SOUNDLY

"Wisdom Requires Processing"

"Most people would sooner die than think; in fact, they do so."
—Bertrand Russell

"For as he thinks within himself, so is he" (Proverbs 23:7).

As we progress on our journey of perspective, we first encountered the step of seeing and opening our eyes to what is going on; yet seeing is not enough. One must think and process what they're seeing and ask how it squares with the truth from God's Word. In this chapter, we will look at four aspects of thinking that begin with the foundation of knowledge, the counterfeits of thinking, how we process time, and finally a perspective on possession of things.

Think Soundly and Purely

Thinking is the next step. Thinking is not merely a process of our intellect; our thinking must begin from God's revelations, wisdom, and principles and then let these shape our thoughts. Thinking is the process that helps us not to be reactive or led by our emotions. God brings soundness to our thought process. Thinking must begin with God's interests and others' interests at heart and ahead of our own. This brings purity to our thinking, which guards us against being selfish.

> *"And the peace of God, which transcends all understanding,*
> *will guard your hearts and your minds in Christ Jesus. Finally,*

> *brothers and sisters, whatever is true, whatever is honorable, whatever is right, whatever is pure, whatever is lovely, whatever is commendable, if there is any excellence and if anything worthy of praise, think about these things. As for the things you have learned and received and heard and seen in me, practice these things, and the God of peace will be with you"* (Philippians 4:7-9).
>
> *"Set your minds on things that are above, not on things that are on earth"* (Colossians 3:2).

Foundation of Knowing

Your foundation will determine your life's lasting fruitfulness. Right foundations lead to right thinking and knowing the Lord, His Word, and His ways. This must be your "first principles."

> *"Everyone then who hears these words of mine and does them will be like a wise man who built his house on the rock. And the rain fell, and the floods came, and the winds blew and beat on that house, but it did not fall, because it had been founded on the rock"* (Matthew 7:24-25).
>
> *"More than that, I count all things to be loss in view of the surpassing value of knowing Christ Jesus my Lord, for whom I have suffered the loss of all things, and count them mere rubbish, so that I may gain Christ"* (Philippians 3:8).

We will look at "knowing the Lord" in five ways:

1. Know Him
2. Know the Word Truth.
3. Know His Love
4. Know God's Will
5. Know God's Promises

Know Him. Knowing the Lord is to know Him by experience in your heart and soul (Philippians 3:10). It is more than head knowledge or facts about the Lord. It involves knowing Him in His character as well as the nature of who He is. Much has been written on this subject, so we will only highlight of few of His attributes to set a context for our thinking. God is Good (Psalm 84:11). God is All-Wise (Romans 11:33-36). God is All-Powerful (Jeremiah 32:17). We get to know the Lord primarily by immersing ourselves in His Word.

What are the implications of knowing the Lord being in control? Just this: the Lord is in full control, yet we have responsibility for our actions and thoughts. We must do our part—it is not "let go and let God." We are to be patient in adversity, thankful in prosperity, and in light of the future have great confidence in the faithfulness of God. Here are three steps of application.

1. **Examine your heart and your life for areas where you are trying to control. Give them to the Lord.**
2. **Express your personal thankfulness and gratefulness to the Lord.**
3. **Ask great questions of yourself and of the Lord to gain guidance.**

Know the Word of Truth. John 17:17 says that God's Word is truth. God's Word is the foundation for all truth. It is 66 books written over 1500 years with amazing consistency and impact. We are called to hear, read, study, memorize, and meditate on it. Most of all we are called to live it out by applying it to our daily lives.

- **Knowing God's Word requires the application that must be focused on pleasing God rather than pleasing others.**
- **Every problem a person has is related to his or her concept of God.**
- **Attitude is as important as action in obeying God's commands.**
- **Application is a process, not a single event.**

Know His Love. We know in our hearts that the "Love of God" is unlimited, undeserved, and unconditional. We can't earn it or lose it. In Matthew 22:37 Christ commands that "*we should love the Lord with all our heart, soul, and mind.*" Our call to love God needs to be the primary thing that should mark my life. Out of this love, we will love ourselves and then love others (the body and the lost).

> *"To know God is to love Him, because the more we grasp—not merely in our minds but in our experience—WHO HE IS and what HE HAS DONE FOR US, the more our hearts will respond in love and gratitude. It is when we respond to this love that we become the people He has called us to be. By God's grace, we need to grow in love with Him in our thoughts, in our emotions, and in our actions."*
>
> —Ken Boa, *Conformed to His Image*

The most important thing about us is not what we do, but who and whose we are in Christ. Being is more fundamental than doing. Relationships must precede relevance or results. Our ultimate source of fulfillment and enjoyment is found in fellowship and intimacy with God out of which flows my functioning.

Know God's Will. Knowing the will of God is to know what pleases Him and what is at His heart. We will give a simple yet profound process to determine God's will and how to follow His calling and leading you in the chapter on Choosing.

Know God's Promises. God's Word is filled with promises from our Creator to provide and deliver. The Bible is the ultimate source of truth and God is faithful to fulfill all his promises. As your read these Bible verses about the promises of God, claim them over your life! These are only a couple of many:

> *"For as many as the promises of God are, in Him they are yes; therefore through Him also is our Amen to the glory of God through us"* (2 Corinthians 1:20).
>
> *"Through these He has granted to us His precious and magnificent promises, so that by them you may become partakers of the divine nature"* (2 Peter 1:4).

Key Principle: Know God, know perspective; No God, no perspective.

> *"Once you become aware that the main business that you are here for is to know God, most of life's problems fall into place of their own accord."*
>
> —J. I. Packer

Counterfeits

There are many false, worldly foundations. These are mirages or trap doors. We need to discern good from evil. We need to think, ask questions, and examine the situation. We need to be careful of false teachers of God's Word as these are like wolves in sheep's clothes.

> *"So I came to hate life because everything done here under the sun is so troubling. Everything is meaningless—like chasing the wind. So what do people get in this life for all their hard work and anxiety? Their days of labor are filled with pain and grief; even at night, their minds cannot rest. It is all meaningless"* (Ecclesiastes 2:17, 22-23 (NLT)).
>
> *"Woe to those who call evil good, and good evil; who substitute darkness for light and light for darkness; who substitute bitter for sweet and sweet for bitter!"* (Isaiah 5:20).

We will consider six primary things that can be lies or counterfeits.

1. **Belongings**
2. **Power, Pleasure, Position**
3. **Satan is the great deceiver.**
4. **Emotions**
5. **Performance-based acceptance**
6. **We battle the flesh, the world, the devil.**

Belongings. Watch out for money or things that give confidence and yet will not last. More money means more responsibility, not more happiness. Don't chase trinkets and tinsel. Give up ownership, be a steward. Money and wealth are morally neutral. The accumulation of goods leads to entanglement, which ties you down and renders you unable to follow the Lord. Many people are making the same mistake Solomon made—thinking that more money and material things are going to bring them happiness.

Power, Pleasure, Position. Humans without the Lord give their lives and souls for these three things. Power is probably the most challenging because, with it, you can do good things, but you can also do bad things. Power without the Lord will always hurt and overrun people. Then there are those who are just seeking pleasure and fun out of life. This is not wrong necessarily, but if that's our total focus, then it will never satisfy us. Then there are those who seek positions or places of power in order to be held in high esteem.

Satan is the great deceiver. Satan is the great deceiver. He is the father of lies and he masquerades as light, yet all he does is bring darkness and death into this world. The schemes of the devil often look good and seem spiritual, but there's always an element of doubt or untruth that is designed to lead you away from the Lord.

Emotions. Emotions and feeling good are often the focus of many people's lives. They just want to be happy, but emotions can give all kinds of false readings, whether they're positive or negative. If we live by our emotions, we will surely be led astray by our emotions. Emotions are great; they help us have deeper relationships and more depth in our understanding and being present for other people. But, they need to be held in check with God's truth and our own reasoning capacity.

Performance-based acceptance. *Performance-based* acceptance is one of the great lies of our world. It says that if I do good, then I will be accepted, be in someone's good graces, or be held in high esteem. This, however, runs counter to the Lord. Performance-based acceptance is a hallmark of the world and is found as a foundation and motivation in the business world, education, and sports. It does motivate to a degree, but this is not the basis of my worth or my value.

We battle the flesh, the world, and the devil. One of the great challenges of counterfeits is that it puts us in a battle against the flesh, the world, and the devil. Our flesh is always wanting to control and get its needs met, so we pursue things that are counter to the Lord or that will draw us away from the Lord. The world also entices us us to pursue its end versus the purposes of the Lord. Finally, the enemy is always seeking to take us off course, whether it's by a few degrees or by 180 degrees.

To overcome these counterfeit challenges, we need to have a grounding in God's Word and a true discernment of God's will. We have to be careful of false teachers or people teaching from the Bible what is either half true or has error in it that will lead us astray. So the application is that we need to know ourselves, we need to know God's Word, and we need to know our culture and our surroundings in order that we would be careful and discerning and not fall into the traps of this world.

Time

Our view of time will change how we see the past, present, and future. Our view of time and eternity will shape our perspective and help determine our actions.

We live in difficult days, and we need to be wise as well as circumspect on how to use our time. Our view of time can be described by two Greek words: *Chronos* time or *Kairos* time. *Chronos* time refers to the days, the hours, and the moments. *Kairos* time is the opportunity times, the God times, and we need to be able to discern the difference, not just go by our calendar or iPhone. We need to be able to look at things from God's perspective as it relates to time. We need to seize the day and make the most of it because the days are evil, and we don't know if we'll have more time ahead of us. So, we have to make every day count. We are encouraged to redeem the time, buy it up, and pay it forward. We will consider six ideas:

1. **Know the times.**
2. **Make the most of your time.**
3. **Waiting on the Lord**
4. **Realize in the last days difficult times will come.**
5. **Busy or putting off the timing of situations**
6. **Eternal versus the temporal nature of things guides and motivates.**

Know the Times. The Bible encourages us to know the times so we will be able to discern what to do. This means that we need to be students of our culture, students of our world, and have a perspective of what's going on so we can know what to do. *"The sons of Issachar, men who understood the times, with knowledge of what Israel should do"* (1 Chronicles 12:32).

Make the Most of your Time. Making the most of your time is one of the most critical aspects of living life. We don't know when our last day will be so we need to treat each day in each moment as if it might be our last. We need to seize the day take hold of it make it work for us we need to redeem the time or buy it back and utilized time as one of the most valuable resources that we have been given. *"So then, be careful how you walk, not as unwise people but as wise, making the most of your time, because the days are evil. Therefore do not be foolish, but understand what the will of the Lord is"* (Ephesians 5:15-17).

Waiting on the Lord. Waiting on the Lord is one of the most difficult things to do. We like to be in control and like to make decisions and take action on our own schedule in time frames. The Lord has a different time frame the Lord has a different schedule and we have to conform to His plans. *"I waited patiently for the Lord; And He reached down to me and heard my cry. He brought me up out of the pit of destruction, out of the mud; and He set my feet on a rock, making my footsteps firm"* (Psalm 40:1-2).

Realize in the last days difficult times will come. When Paul wrote to Timothy in his very last letter, he encouraged Timothy to realize that in the last days difficult times will come and not to be surprised about the challenges and the difficulties of the world. In fact, as the end time approaches, things will become more difficult and more challenging. Indeed, we may face more persecution and more difficulty. *"But realize this, that in the last days difficult times will come"* (2 Timothy 3:1).

Busy or Putting off the timing of situations. One of the great challenges that we do face is that we live in a world that loves and promotes busyness. We are often rushing around going from one thing to the next without considering slowing down or other alternatives. This "worshiping of busyness" always leads to a less fruitful outcome.

Consider the following quotes on time. These help us to think beyond the moment.

> *"I wish it need not have happened in my time," said Frodo. "So do I," said Gandalf, "and so do all who live to see such times. But that is not for them to decide. All we have to decide is what to do with the time that is given us."*
> —J. R. R. Tolkien

> *"Life is short. Focus on what really matters most. You have to change your priorities over time."*
> —Roy T. Bennett

> *"Time is precious, but truth is more precious than time."*
> —Benjamin Disraeli

> *"Time is what we want most, but what we use worst."*
> —William Penn

> *"It's not that we have little time, but more that we waste a good deal of it."*
>
> —Seneca

Possessions

True perspective is found outside of ourselves, yet it must be personalized to make a difference. A proper view of self can only be from God's view of us and how He made us. We need the "Mind of Christ."

Our following Christ comes from our possessions in Christ. It is threefold: our intimate relationship with Christ, our provision of being made new "in Christ," and when He is our source of life, power, and wisdom that comes from the Spirit. We are called to "follow first": *"Seek first the Kingdom God and His righteousness"* (Matthew 6:33). Our relationship with the Lord is not founded on the performance-based acceptance of achieving.

***"Christ is the vine, we are the branches and apart from Him, we can do nothing"* (John 15:5).**

- His Love makes us Whole. (See 2 Corinthians 5:17.)
- His Love meets our Deepest Needs (See Philippians 4:19.)
- Receiving His Love allows us to love God and others which grows us in the process. (See Ephesians 3:14-19.)

We have every spiritual blessing in Him (See Ephesians 1:3.)

- Christ lives in us. (See Galatians 2:20, Colossians 1:27).
- His indwelling spirit is our hope and provides us with everything we need for Him to use us.
- We have this power in earthen vessels. (See 2 Corinthians 4:7.)
- Christ in us is the source of hope and leaders bring hope to others.

1. Intimacy with Christ restores us to the completeness and being made whole. Fruit is borne out of this intimacy. We first receive His love and then love him and others. (See Romans 6:1-8.)
2. Our new Identity in Christ provides us with security, significance, and satisfaction. (See Ephesians 1:3-10.)

3. His Indwelling Spirit offers Life, power, wisdom, and vision; this is a lifelong growth process. (See John 10:10.) *"To me, the very least of all saints, this grace was given, to preach to the Gentiles the unfathomable riches of Christ"* (Ephesians 3:8).

> *"Therefore if anyone is in Christ, this person is a new creation; the old things passed away; behold, new things have come. Therefore, if anyone is in Christ, this person is a new creation; the old things passed away; behold, new things have come"* (2 Corinthians 5:17).

Our Identity in Christ is a truth that will define us, shape us, and then compel us. Too often we believe the lies of the world and the enemy, which is disastrous.

Christ lives in me. Christ living in me means the Holy Spirit is working out His life through me; this indwelling Spirit is the source of life, wisdom, and power. And apart from Christ, we are incapable of living the Christian life. This indwelling Spirit allows me to live free, to be vulnerable, to follow the Lord ,and to be used by the Lord in his Kingdom purposes. Christ in us is our source of life, hope, wisdom, and power.

1. Christ produces hope in us that becomes a ministry to others.
2. We move from trying to be "like" Christ to receiving the "life" of Christ.

We have everything for life and godliness.

> *"One of the dangers of having a lot of money is that you may be quite satisfied with the kinds of happiness money can give, and so fail to realize your need for God. In other words, it is hard for those who are rich in this sense to enter the kingdom."*
>
> —C. S. Lewis

Application

Thinking Soundly – 8 Ground Rules for Living

1. **Life has a 100% mortality rate.** *Death awaits us all. Get busy living or get busy dying. Life is short, make every day count.*

2. **Without the Lord, life is vanity.** *We are made for another world. There is no full satisfaction on earth. Examine actions and priorities.*

3. **The Lord declares man to be worthy.** *He gives us Identity and significance. Contentment, peace, and joy are found in Christ.*

4. **We have a new life in Christ.** *Only Christ can give us eternal life, transform us, and change us. We grow as we follow and He works.*

5. **We are not in control. God is in full control of life and circumstances.** *We can control our attitudes and motives.*

6. **God gives man work to do.** *We fulfill a God-given purpose. He gives us meaning. We don't retire from God's work.*

7. **Invest in what Jesus invested: the things of eternity.** *Focus your life to God's Word and to spiritually growing people.*

8. **What we do on earth directly impacts our eternity.** *Our rewards and treasure is in heaven and are given on the basis of faithfulness to opportunity.*

Now What?

> *"Who has known the mind of the Lord so as to instruct him?" But we have the mind of Christ"* (1 Corinthians 2:16).
>
> *"That I may know Him and the power of His resurrection and the fellowship of His sufferings, being conformed to His death"* (Philippians 3:10).

- **Get to know the Lord** – who He is, what He does, where He is guiding.

» Read the Psalms.

» Put the Word in your heart.

» Ask for His wisdom to process.

- **Think Christianly.**

  » Apply a first principles mindset.

  » Live with open-handed hospitality.

  » Build relational networks.

  » Seek a deep commitment to the gospel's significance in culture.

- **Ask questions.**

  » Be curious. Consider under the surface and beyond the present.

- **Give up ownership and become a steward.**

  » Be generous and give.

  » Consider your reward in heaven.

- **TIME – Live today.** Learn from the past without being stuck. Consider the future without being trapped.

  » Be at rest, slow down.

- **Take hold of and appropriate Christ.**

  » Consider your identity in Christ.

  » Believe you are adopted, blessed, and wealthy.

Know God, know hope/peace/perspective. No God, no hope/peace/perspective.

> **OBSERVATIONS:** *The satisfaction we have is found in Christ alone. Don't believe everything your see and hear on the surface, think. Think twice, act once. Life without Christ is meaningless, vanity of vanity. Remember your foundation.*

As we conclude this sub-chapter on thinking, here are some quotes to ponder.

"One of the most efficient ways you can improve your life is by simply thinking in a more positive way."
—Robert Norman

"Thinking too little about things or thinking too much both make us obstinate and fanatical."
—Blaise Pascal

"Whether you think you can, or you think you can't—you're right."
—Henry Ford

"Simple can be harder than complex: You have to work hard to get your thinking clean to make it simple. But it's worth it in the end because once you get there, you can move mountains."
—Steve Jobs

Chapter 4 (c)

SURRENDER FULLY

"Fit to Quit"

"If anyone wishes to come after Me, he must deny himself, and take up his cross daily and follow Me" (Luke 9:23).

Being *"Fit to Quit"* is an expression that describes coming to the end of your resources and having nowhere else to turn. This is actually a good thing in the Christian life when we come to the end of our own human, fleshly resources. We no longer rely upon what we can do for the Lord, but we come to a place of dying to self.

The Power of Perspective comes from the life, and leadership of Jesus Christ being released only through our brokenness and surrender.

Here's one of the most amazing truths in the Bible: If you know Jesus Christ as your Savior, He lives in you! Carefully read Galatians 2:20. *"I have been crucified with Christ; and it is no longer I who live, but Christ lives in me; and the life which I now live in the flesh I live by faith in the Son of God who loved me and gave Himself up for me."*

The Lord is looking for followers who are different: Followers who don't rely upon their charisma, education, hard work, intellect, abilities, and skills. The Lord is not interested in followers who have a lukewarm allegiance to God, relying primarily on their strength and willpower to make things happen in business. He is searching for people who are different inside and out.

Matthew 23:10-12 says, *"Do not be called leaders; for One is your Leader, that is, Christ. But the greatest among you shall be your servant.*

Whoever exalts himself shall be humbled; and whoever humbles himself shall be exalted." Stop for a moment, and let that sink in. **There is only one leader, and it is not you!** Christ invites you to submit to Him as Lord and allow Him to lead through your life.

Just as all spiritual life flows from Christ, so all godliness flows from Him alone who is the Leader in us. In John 15:5 Jesus said, *"I am the vine, you are the branches; he who abides in Me and I in him, he bears much fruit, for apart from Me you can do nothing."* How much can you really accomplish apart from Christ? Nothing! Zero! True God-honoring leadership does not come from our own limited human resources, but from His unlimited supernatural resources.

Many leaders who know Christ want to do things for Him, as if He needs our help, our paycheck, or our expertise. The leadership that God is interested in is His leadership *through* us, rather than our work and leadership *for* Him. This type of leadership flows out of a person's vibrant, intimate relationship with God.

Unconditional Surrender

On September 4, 1945, World War II in the Pacific officially ended when Japan unconditionally surrendered to General Douglas MacArthur and the Allies on the *U.S.S. Missouri.* In war, unconditional surrender involves the defeated submitting fully to the will of the victorious. The vanquished have no choice.

We who know Christ are called to surrender our will unconditionally to the Lord. God, however, has given us the freedom to choose whether to surrender. Unlike the vanquished in war, our decision to surrender is motivated by the Lord's unconditional love for us. Our surrender is an act of worship. *"Therefore, I urge you, brothers, in view of God's mercy, to offer your bodies as living and sacrifices, holy and pleasing to God—this is your spiritual act of worship"* (Romans 12:1, NIV).

Christian leaders have long recognized the importance of this total surrender. Dwight L. Moody, the founder of the Moody Bible Institute, once said, "The world has yet to see what can happen through a person fully committed to doing God's will." Dawson Trotman, founder of the Navigators, added, "God can do more through one person who is 100 percent committed to Him, than through 99 who are only partially committed."

The primary requirement of a godly follower is unconditional surrender to follow and obey the Lord as an empty, clean vessel for His use.

Jesus Christ Modeled Surrender.

In the life of Christ, we see that he completely humbled and submitted himself to his Heavenly Father, so that God was free to work powerfully through Him. Here are some examples of Christ humbling Himself to His Father. Note how Jesus used the words *nothing* and *not* referring to Himself.

> *"The Son can do* **nothing** *of Himself"* (John 5:19).
>
> *"I [Jesus] can do* **nothing** *of My own initiative, as I hear, I judge; and My judgment is just; because I do not seek My own will but the will of Him who sent Me"* (John 5:30).

Are You Willing to Surrender?

Jesus was willing to surrender to God, and He tells us in Luke 9:23, *"If anyone wishes to come after Me, he must deny Himself, and take up his cross daily and follow Me."*

It requires nothing less than a transformation of our hearts to submit to Christ as Lord and as the Leader of our business life. Because of our own pride and the world's perspective of leadership that is so deeply ingrained in most of us, it can require years and often difficult circumstances to completely humble ourselves and embrace God's way of leadership.

God knows everything about you, and He is constantly thinking about you. *"You have searched me, Lord, and you know me. You know when I sit and when I rise...you are familiar with all my ways. Before a word is on my tongue you, Lord, know it completely...Your eyes saw my unformed body; all the days ordained for me were written in your book before one of them came to be. How precious to me are your thoughts, God! How vast is the sum of them! Were I to count them, they would outnumber the grains of sand"* (Psalm 139:1-4, 16-18, NIV).

The Lord not only knows you perfectly, but because of His great love for you, He wants the best for you. Jeremiah 29:11-13 tells us, *"'For I know the plans I have for you,' declares the Lord, 'plans to prosper you and not harm you, plans to give you hope and a future.'"* Our Heavenly Father knows what we need to become His leader. He understands that sometimes our character is best developed in adversity. The circumstances may be difficult, painful and lonely, but they are intended to draw us into a deeper relationship with Christ.

We have a choice. We can respond by either accepting and learning, or fighting and fleeing. It is in our struggle that of our complete dependence on Christ alone, and learn to submit to our Lord and allow Him to live His life through us.

In the 1600s, Francois Fenelon, wrote a letter to his friends in prison that capture this understanding:

> *I cannot express to you how deeply I sympathize with you in your time of suffering. I suffer right along with you, but still, it cheers me up to know that God loves you.*
>
> *And the very proof that God loves you is that He does not spare you, but lays upon you the cross of Jesus Christ. Whatever spiritual knowledge or feelings we may have, they are all a delusion if they do not lead us to the real and constant practice of dying to self. And it is true that we do not die without suffering. Nor is it possible to be considered truly dead while there is any part of us which is yet alive.*
>
> *This spiritual death (which is really a blessing in disguise) is undeniably painful. It cuts "swift and deep into our innermost thoughts and desires with all their parts, exposing us for what we really are." The great Physician, who sees in us what we cannot see, knows exactly where to place the knife. He cuts away that which we are most reluctant to give up. And how it*

> *hurts! But we must remember that pain is only felt where there is life, and where there is life is just the place where death is needed.*

The Bible leaves no doubt as to the necessity of brokenness. Consider some of the evidence:

- **King David** lived life to the fullest—sometimes too full. Among other sins, we know that he suffered from lust, engaged in adultery, and was guilty of murder. In order to grab David's attention and teach him the seriousness of what he had willfully done, God allowed David's marriage to dissolve, his baby died, and his older children rebelled against him. David was a man after God's heart, but God had to break him. (See 2 Samuel 11-15.)

- **The apostle Paul** was a brilliant scholar and skilled debater. But he suffered from hatred (of Christians) and pride. God loved Paul enough to break him through blindness, beatings, imprisonment, mistrust, questions about his standing as an apostle, and public humiliation. (See Acts 9, 2 Corinthians 6:4-12.)

- **Jonah** was a reluctant and disobedient prophet. He heard and refused the call of God, preferring to let his enemies experience God's harsh judgment. Jonah's self-centeredness and lack of compassion toward fellow sinners resulted in a life marked by emotional turmoil, physical peril, and public rejection. (See Jonah 1-3.)

- **Moses** was a highly educated orphan, raised in a privileged environment to prepare for leadership. But after breaking away from his Egyptian setting, he returned to lead God's people. Unfortunately, in one particular circumstance he disobeyed God and beat a rock with a stick, ostensibly taking credit for a miracle God performed by generating water from that stone. That act of defiance displayed the level of pride and anger residing within Moses. In response, God allowed Israel's leader to complete the work of leading the Jews to the brink of the Promised Land but banned Moses from entering it. (See Numbers 20.)

Key Principles

1. **Worry, anxiousness, fear, and anger are signs we have taken back the reigns of our life or have not fully surrendered. Peace, joy, and grace are signs that we have surrendered.**

> *"Be anxious for nothing, but in everything by prayer and supplication let your prayers be made known to God, the peace of God which surpasses all knowledge will guard your hearts and minds in Christ Jesus"* (Philippians 4:6-7).

Surrender is not a one-time event; it is a daily ongoing process of giving up. As we mature and grow spiritually, we discover new areas (and maybe old areas we have taken back) that are not under the Lordship of Christ. This lack of surrender results in our being worried, fearful, tied up in knots, and even lashing out in anger. When we find that we can't control people or circumstances the flesh (desire to control) kicks in.

It is good to examine areas of worry, fear, and/or anger as signs that may need to be surrendered.

As we surrender, we will experience the peace, joy, and fruit of Christ as He manifests Himself through us.

2. **Brokenness is God's means to bring us to our own end, to gain our attention. Brokenness is not surrender.**

The Lord has to break each of us as humans of our reliance on our natural resources, strengths, and abilities as well as our flesh (meeting my needs my way) and our sins/disobedience. God has to correct and/or chastise (pick us up and clean us) in order that we maybe in a place to bear fruit.

Brokenness quite often involves pain (physical, emotional, and spiritual). Silence from the Lord can bring us to our end. God even uses pruning (no fault of our own) to bring us to our end. Brokenness can happen in our spirit, soul (emotions and relationships), and in our physical body (sickness and disease).

Brokenness comes also from loss, hurts, damaged emotions, and being empty. The enemy will also bring us to our end by attacking and deceiving us (the story of Job). The world will let us down in the end because it cannot satisfy our needs. Brokenness can come from our failures, struggles, and trials—all of which can overwhelm us.

Brokenness is God's way to bring us a crossroad where we either surrender by choice or to continue fighting. People can be broken and never surrender in their spirit or heart.

God does not waste pain but uses it to prepare us, to gain our attention, to bring us to dependence, and to identify with His hurt and that of Jesus Christ.

- *Brokenness is the first step to fruitfulness.* (See John 12:24.)
- *Brokenness is the beginning of God's means of maturing us.* (See James 1:2-4.)
- *Brokenness is a means of ministry so we become broken bread and poured out wine.* (See 2 Corinthians 1:3-4.)

God is opposed to the proud and gives grace to the humble (broken).

Proud People	Broken People
Focus on the failure of others	Overwhelmed with a sense of their own spiritual need
A critical, fault-finding spirit; looking at everyone else's faults with a microscope, but their own with a telescope	Compassionate; can forgive much because they know how much they have been forgiven
Self-righteous; look down on others	Esteem all others better than themselves
Independent, self-sufficient spirit	Have a dependent spirit; recognize a need for others

Have to prove they are right; Claim rights; have a demanding spirit	Willing to yield the right to be right
Self-protective of their time, their rights, and their reputation	Self-denying
Desire to be served	Motivated to serve others
Desire to be a success	Motivated to make others a success
Have a drive to be recognized and appreciated	Have a sense of their own unworthiness; thrilled that God would use them at all
Wounded when others are promoted, and they are overlooked	Eager for others to get the credit, rejoice when others are lifted up
Have a subconscious feeling that this ministry is privileged to have them and their gifts	Heart attitude is, "I don't deserve to have a part of this ministry"
Think of what they can do for God	Know they have nothing to offer God except Jesus flowing through their broken lives

God uses the pain and difficulty of life to break us of ourselves and pride. He requires us to choose to surrender to Him and His ways.

3.   **Surrendering places us in dependence on the Lord's will and His way. We are to die quick and die often.**

The Lord wants to rule and reign in our lives, this can only happen when we decrease, die to self, yield, and humble ourselves to the Lord's will rather than our own will. Death to self is putting our flesh patterns to death, letting God have authority in those areas.

> *"And He was saying to them all, 'If anyone wishes to come after Me, he must deny himself, and take up his cross daily and follow Me'"* (Luke 9:23).

> *"And he who does not take his cross and follow after Me is not worthy of Me. He who has found his life will lose it, and he who has lost his life for My sake will find it. He who receives you receives Me, and he who receives Me receives Him who sent Me"* (Matthew 10:38-40).

- **Surrender of:** our resources, possessions, our will, desires, dreams, idols, hurts, wrongs, emotions, our mind
- **Surrender to:** God's sovereignty, His authority, His control, His love
- **How to surrender:**
  - » Submit—give up control of outcomes and our perceived gain.
  - » Acknowledge our weakness and our falling short.
  - » Wholly and fully desire God's will in all circumstances.
  - » Surrender daily.
  - » Know that we can't and only He can.
  - » Recognize our flesh patterns and offer them to the Lord.
  - » Serve others.
  - » Relinquish the world.
  - » Repent of sin.
  - » Restore broken relationships—make the first move.
  - » Receive God's grace and mercy.
  - » Rely on God in the spiritual battles.

What surrender looks like: (a good and biblical sense) slave, servant, obscure, humble.

4. **The releasing of Christ and His power comes through our weakness, emptiness, and being made clean.**

It is only in our emptiness, weakness, and being clean (pure) that we are available for God to use us. There are two biblical pictures—branch and vessel. The vine (life) flows through the branch in order to bear fruit. The second picture is that of a vessel that is used to serve. It is filled to overflowing. Both are vital to the process, yet life does not come from them; they are simply tools that God uses.

Another picture is that we are a dam with a whole reservoir behind us, and the life from the water and power comes only when it is released as the dam breaks or the spillways are opened.

The goal is not to hold onto or hoard what we have in Christ. He is infinite, and when we give Him away, we still have the whole thing.

> *"Because of the surpassing greatness of the revelations, for this reason, to keep me from exalting myself, there was given me a thorn in the flesh, a messenger of Satan to torment me— to keep me from exalting myself! Concerning this I implored the Lord three times that it might leave me. And He has said to me, 'My grace is sufficient for you, for power is perfected in weakness.' Most gladly, therefore, I will rather boast about my weaknesses, so that the power of Christ may dwell in me. Therefore I am well content with weaknesses, with insults, with distresses, with persecutions, with difficulties, for Christ's sake; for when I am weak, then I am strong"* (2 Corinthians 12:7-10).

5. Molding and shaping our character

Recognizing and embracing God's process of molding us begins with a view that God always has our best interests at heart, He is never unaware, and He is forever in control. He is shaping us outwardly to who we are inwardly. He wants us to work out what He is working in.

> *"And not only this, but we also exult in our tribulations, knowing that tribulation brings about perseverance; and perseverance, proven character; and proven character, hope; and hope does not disappoint, because the love of God has been poured out within our hearts through the Holy Spirit who was given to us"* (Romans 5:3-5).

> *"Consider it all joy, my brethren, when you encounter various trials, knowing that the testing of your faith produces endurance. And let endurance have its perfect result, so that you may be perfect and complete, lacking in nothing"* (James 1:2-4).

> *"In this you greatly rejoice, even though now for a little while, if necessary, you have been distressed by various trials, so that the proof of your faith, being more precious than gold which is perishable, even though tested by fire, may be found to result in praise and glory and honor at the revelation of Jesus Christ"* (1 Peter 1:6-7).

> *"God will develop your character to match your assignment. God does not give big things to little character. What is God doing to develop your character? What you become, God can pass it on, you can't pass on what you don't possess."*
>
> —Henry Blackaby

What character looks like: trustworthiness, integrity, respect, responsibility, caring.

The nature of character in our lives is an obedient heart. It is a desire to *be* pleasing to God and to *do* the will of God in all things.

6. Victory in Surrender

God's great desire is not to defeat us but to use us in His battles and plan. As we surrender to Him, we now are a part of the winning team, and the certain victory is His. It comes only when He leads through us.

> *"But thanks be to God, who always leads us in triumph in Christ, and manifests through us the sweet aroma of the knowledge of Him in every place. For we are a fragrance of Christ to God among those who are being saved and among those who are perishing"* (2 Corinthians 2:14-15).

What does the victory look like?

Know Christ in His sufferings: *"That I may know Him and the power of His resurrection and the fellowship of His sufferings, being conformed to His death"* (Philippians 3:10).

Hear God and Listen to His direction: *"Guard your steps as you go to the house of God and draw near to listen rather than to offer the sacrifice of fools; for they do not know they are doing evil. Do not be hasty in word or impulsive in thought to bring up a matter in the presence of God. For God is in heaven and you are on the earth; therefore let your words be few"* (Ecclesiastes 5:1-2).

Hope is clarified in difficulty: *"Remember the word to Your servant, In which You have made me hope. This is my comfort in my affliction, That Your word has revived me"* (Psalm 119:49-50).

Ministry comes out of pain: *"Blessed be the God and Father of our Lord Jesus Christ, the Father of mercies and God of all comfort, who comforts us in all our affliction so that we will be able to comfort those who are in any affliction with the comfort with which we ourselves are comforted by God"* (2 Corinthians 1:3-4).

The victory and reward await us: *"For I consider that the sufferings of this present time are not worthy to be compared with the glory that is to be revealed to us. For the anxious longing of the creation waits eagerly for the revealing of the sons of God"* (Romans 8:18-19).

Christ prays for us in our weakness: *"In the same way the Spirit also helps our weakness; for we do not know how to pray as we should, but the*

Spirit Himself intercedes for us with groanings too deep for words; and He who searches the hearts knows what the mind of the Spirit is, because He intercedes for the saints according to the will of God" (Romans 8:26-27).

We are conformed to His image, *"And we know that God causes all things to work together for good to those who love God, to those who are called according to His purpose. For those whom He foreknew, He also pre-destined to become conformed to the image of His Son, so that He would be the firstborn among many brethren"* (Romans 8:28-29).

> *God is and always will be victorious. He uses our giving up to conform us to His image. Surrender is the pivot upon which the fullness of Christ is realized and few truly experience. The entering into God's goodness comes only as a volitional choice on our part.*

To enter into the goodness of what Christ offers and His victory, we must choose to surrender. This is a step of faith and an entering into the unknown where we lose control. This is exactly where God wants us and then can use us.

We must submit and come under His authority if we are to be available for His use. The biblical word is "come."

> *"Come to Me, all who are weary and heavy-laden, and I will give you rest. Take My yoke upon you and learn from Me, for I am gentle and humble in heart, and you will find rest for your souls. For My yoke is easy and My burden is light"* (Matthew 11:28-30).
>
> *"Jesus said to him, 'If you wish to be complete, go and sell your possessions and give to the poor, and you will have treasure in heaven; and come, follow Me'"* (Matthew 19:21).

> *"Jesus stood and cried out, saying, 'If anyone is thirsty, let him come to Me and drink. He who believes in Me, as the Scripture said, 'From his innermost being will flow rivers of living water'"* (John 7:37-38).

The following is a chart that summarizes key ideas about surrender.

Surrender			
Posture	**Process**	**Product**	**Outcome**
Yielded	Acknowledge and	Hope is clarified	Releases the
Repentance	repent from sin	Molds our	power of Christ
Conformed	Brokenness and	character	Witness to the
Broken	pain due to self or	Develops purity	world
Humbled	others	Creates	Defeats the
Persecuted	Spiritual Battle with	dependence	enemy
Transformed	World, Flesh, Devil	Brings humility	Builds community
Sacrifice	Emotional hurt in	Enhances need	Multiplies the
Weakness	relationships	for others	church
Decrease	Persecution	Value one	Grows our
Let go of control	Trials and Struggles	another	ministry
Give Up	Worn out and spent	Become available	Allows God to
Every knee bows	Disease	Obedience grows	show up
	Wars	Experience	
		comfort of God	

Discussion:

1. Why and how does God use trials, struggles, and pain in our life?
2. What is God allowing you to go through, and what is the lesson He is teaching?
3. How does brokenness and surrender integrate in the world's approach to leading?
4. How are hope and pain related, and why is this significant to leadership?

Chapter 4 (d)

DECIDE BOLDLY

"The Product of Your Choices"

"Everything can be taken away from a man but one thing: the last of the human freedom—to choose one's attitude in any given set of circumstances, to choose one's own way."
—Viktor Frankl

Decision-Making

Seeing and thinking lead to making decisions about the choices in front of us. Decision-making is a normal part of life where we make daily choices, many small ones and some large ones. What is the process and what are the results of making those decisions? This all relates to perspective. This decision-making must be done with sincerity and wisdom such that both the process and product glorify the Lord. We will first consider this in four ways: choices, process, alignment, and outcome.

Choices

We all have choices in life. We don't control the circumstances of our lives—good or bad—but we can control and decide on our motives, choices, and attitudes—whether they are positive or negative. That is called the perspective of decision-making.

One of first hurdles in life is to understand who is in control. It's only from that perspective that we are able to know what we can control and what we can't control. The Lord is in full control of all things, nothing escapes His view or His power.

To give up control as a Christian is to allow God to be in charge of the results and how He wants to unfold the process. Out part is to thank Him, trust Him, and rest in Him in spite of the pain, hurt, and loss in the moment. Giving up control on our part does not mean we won't hurt, grieve, and experience loss. It is in our tears that we know God's love and presence. Giving up control is not "letting go and letting God." We will be held accountable for our thoughts and our subsequent steps of faith.

Process: Count the Cost, Pay the Price, Reap the Reward.

Count the Cost

Don't give yourself to mediocrity, shallowness, vanity, striving after the wind. As we walk with the Lord we must also count the cost. One of the best passages for this is found in Luke 14:26-35.

> *"If anyone comes to Me, and does not hate his own father and mother and wife and children and brothers and sisters, yes, and even his own life, he cannot be My disciple. Whoever does not carry his own cross and come after Me cannot be My disciple. For which one of you, when he wants to build a tower, does not first sit down and calculate the cost to see if he has enough to complete it?*
>
> *"Otherwise, when he has laid a foundation and is not able to finish, all who observe it begin to ridicule him, saying, 'This man began to build and was not able to finish.' Or what king, when he sets out to meet another king in battle, will not first sit down and consider whether he is strong enough with ten thousand men to encounter the one coming against him with twenty thousand? Or else, while the other is still far away, he sends a delegation and asks for terms of peace.*
>
> *"So then, none of you can be My disciple who does not give up all his own possessions. Therefore, salt is good; but if even salt has become tasteless, with what will it be seasoned? It is useless either for the soil or for the manure pile; it is thrown out. He who has ears to hear, let him hear."*

Counting the Cost – Luke 14:26-36

The following are observations we see from this passage.

1. Love Christ so much that any other love appears as hate. (RELATIONSHIPS)
2. Carry our own Cross and come after Christ. (PURPOSE)
3. Give up all our own possessions. (POSSESSIONS)

If you "Count the Cost" you will then need to decide either to invest in eternity and reap the reward, or pay the price now and never have anything to show. Note the product of "reaping the reward" and "paying the price."

Consequences:

Reap the Reward Eternally and Enjoy His Riches Now and Forever.

1. Love – It is not that we should not love, we must love in the right order.
2. Hope – Hope is the ultimate motivation and will animate our faith.
3. Faith – Faith pleases the Lord and encourages others to do likewise.

Stewardship is at the heart of all three opportunities.

Pay the Price Now and Have Nothing Forever.

1. You will not finish, but instead you will go out of business and suffer the shame of others.
2. You will stop short and compromise with the enemy. He wins and you have nothing.
3. You become useless and discarded. You will lose out on experiencing God and His power. There will be a loss of reward.

Alignment

"So then, be careful how you walk, not as unwise people but as wise, making the most of your time, because the days are evil. Therefore do not be foolish, but understand what the will of the Lord is" (Ephesians 5:15-17).

Alignment involves our personal posture which connects with the Lord in humility to listen and receive. When our hearts are right, then we can align ourselves with God's Word and prayer. We then seek counsel. Alighment of these areas provides wisdom. We continue in alignment by looking outward to recognize our circumstances how they fit with God's Kingdom purposes. We confirm the alignment process by connecting these above insights with our purpose. The final confirmation is peace in our heart.

Personal Posture:	Intimacy and Neutrality	Listen and Receive
Spiritual Guidance:	Word, Prayer, and Counsel	Wisdom and Apply
Navigational Markers:	Circumstances and Kingdom	Watching and Focusing
Final Approach:	Purpose and Peace	Hope and Commitment

Intimacy and Neutrality

Being with Jesus is a matter of Intimacy and quietness. How are you doing in your walk? We are called to "abide" in Christ from John 15:5. We need to keep consulting Jesus from beginning to end in our decisions. What hinders you from doing this? What could you do differently, in practice or attitude, to maintain and even deepen your connection with Him along the way?

Surrender is to die quick , die often, and die fully. It is maturity, humility, and wisdom. *"Trust in the Lord with all your heart; do not depend on your own understanding. Seek his will in all you do, and he will show you which path to take"* (Proverbs 3:5-6 NLT). "Getting Neutral" is the challenge of dying to self and wanting God's desires over your own. Be honest with God and yourself about how much you actually want His preference in your decision-making.

Word, Prayer, and Counsel

Pray, read, gain counsel. Slow down, ask, listen. Consider one decision you are trying to make. *"Every part of Scripture is God-breathed and useful one way or another—showing us truth, exposing our rebellion, correcting our mistakes, training us to live God's way. Through the Word we are put together and shaped up for the tasks God has for us"* (2 Timothy 3:16-17 MSG) The two sources to help people gather the facts: the Bible, and the wise counsel of experts and mature believers. What measures have you taken to gather facts pertaining to your decision?

Circumstances and Kingdom

Keep your eyes open. Be patient and pay attention. *"We can make our plans, but the Lord determines our steps"* (Proverbs 16:9). What is the difference between you making plans and the Lord determining your steps? Facts are more finite and objective; circumstances require that we pay attention to the unfolding story. What circumstances are happening around you that are inviting you to pay attention? What might they be revealing to you?

Purpose and Peace

When we have received and clearly defined our purpose as from God, it will have a dramatic effect on how we live our life day to day. We will be able to rest and enjoy God's working through us in miraculous ways. We will experience fruit and joy like we have never known. Our lives will be characterized by peace and contentment. Although having a purpose does not mean a pain-free life, one without difficulty or struggle. Quite the contrary, we may experience more trials and difficulties when we walk with God, yet He never leaves us or forsakes us.

Peace is the final confirmation. *"Do not be anxious about anything, but in everything by prayer and pleading with thanksgiving let your requests be made known to God. And the peace of God, which surpasses all comprehension, will guard your hearts and minds in Christ Jesus"* (Philippians 4:6-7).

Outcome

Faith and Fruit

Our spiritual growth is comprised of three different elements. On a personal level we walk by faith, which produces maturity and wisdom with the outworking of the fruit of the Spirit. The second element is healthy relationships, which are characterized by unity and others being edified and built up. The third element of our spiritual growth begins to become outward looking and missional. It has a focus on the Kingdom and having impact within God's Kingdom.

Faith – Walk, Maturity

As we grow in making godly decisions, our innermost being develops godly character. This character is produced by Christ's transformation of our hearts and our minds as we give up control and allow Him to rule and reign in our life. To walk with the Lord is a process and a journey. It's not an event nor is it something that takes place quickly. It is the product of intimacy and contentment and an inner peace which come from Christ living in and through us. As we walk we will go through ups and downs, mountains and valleys, in our life. The Lord uses these challenges as well as the good times to grow us and to reveal His will to us and conform us to His image.

Fruit – Kingdom Impact, Changed lives

Kingdom Impact: A godly perspective fulfills our purpose and changes the world. We join the Lord in His purposes and see Him bring Kingdom Impact through our faithfulness. Keep seeking and expanding the Kingdom. Maintain a healthy fear of God.

Changed lives

We are called to have an outward focus of serving others. The Christian life is not self-serving but others-serving. We serve others by the ministry of evangelism and discipleship. We serve others also by helping them in their walk with the Lord and making His truth and ways applicable. When we serve others well, it will produce unified and harmonious relationships.

APPLICATION

Choosing and Making Decisions

We will look at four areas.

1. **Framework:** *A godly wisdom.*
2. **Product:** *Maturity, eternity, peace, joy, fruit*
3. **Relationships:** *Love, care, and serve others more than ourselves.*
4. **Kingdom Impact:** *A godly purpose and influence beyond ourselves. Seeking the Kingdom invites the Lord's presence.*

Framework: A godly process will help us make mature and wise decisions, which in turn helps us grow spiritually and develop contentment and humility to keep us balanced in faith.

Terry Looper in his book, *Sacred Pace*, articulates a four-step process that helps Christians learn how to make wise decisions. Much of this is similar to the ideas above. The consistency helps them know and apply this process well by:

- slowing down their decision-making under the guidance of the Holy Spirit,
- sifting through their surface desires and sinful patterns in order to receive clear, peace-filled answers from the Lord,
- gaining the confident assurance that God's answers are His way of fulfilling the true desires he has placed in their hearts, and grow closer to the One who loves them most and knows them best.

Going about life at a sacred pace involves four simple steps:

1. **Consult your Friend Jesus.** Intimacy and quiet with the Lord.
2. **Gather the facts.** Pray, read, gain counsel.
3. **Watch for circumstances.** Keep your eyes open.
4. **Get neutral.** Decide to surrender, die to self, trust the Lord with the outcome.

Consult your Friend Jesus.

Being with Jesus is a matter of intimacy and quietness. How are you doing in your walk? We are called to "abide" in Christ from John 15:5. The Sacred Pace process encourages us to keep consulting Jesus from beginning to end in our decisions. What hinders you from doing this? What could you do differently, in practice or attitude, to maintain and even deepen your connection with Him along the way.

Gather the facts.

Pray, read, gain counsel. Slow down, ask, listen. Consider one decision you are trying to make. "Every part of Scripture is God-breathed and useful one way or another—showing us truth, exposing our rebellion, correcting our mistakes, training us to live God's way. Through the Word we are put together and shaped up for the tasks God has for us" (2 Timothy 3:16-17 MSG). Sacred Pace mentions three sources to help people gather the facts: the Bible, the truth of who we are, and the wise counsel of experts and mature believers. List what measures you have taken to gather facts pertaining to your decision. Are you missing any of the three sources?

Watch for circumstances.

Keep your eyes open. Be patient and pay attention. We can make our plans, but the Lord determines our steps. (See Proverbs 16:9.) What is the difference between you making plans and the Lord determining your steps? "Facts are more finite and objective; circumstances require that we pay attention to the unfolding story." What circumstances are happening around you that are inviting you to pay attention? What might they be revealing to you?"

Get neutral.

Surrender is to die quick, die often, and die fully. It is maturity, humility, and wisdom. "Trust in the Lord with all your heart; do not depend on your own understanding. Seek his will in all you do, and he will show you which path to take" (Proverbs 3:5–6 NLT). *"Getting Neutral" as the challenge of dying to self and wanting God's desires over your own. Be honest with God and yourself about how much you actually want His preference in your decision-making.*

Decide. Follow. Step out in Faith. Pursue your Calling. These steps build upon one another and continually work together in the trust of this truth:

- God sees the future, and I don't.
- God knows best, and I just think I do.
- God loves me and the people in my life more than I ever can.

As you continue to actively pray, gather, watch, and get neutral, may you know God's peace, letting it fill you deeply.

Be Decisive

As we hear from the Lord, we are called to be decisive in our decision-making process. The following are three ways in which we apply this process.

- **Wisdom over Precision** – Gain input, Analyze, Be Committed, Have Conviction, Analysis/Paralysis, Make the Complex Simple – find the core, Give a voice not a vote, Communicate
- **Make Fewer Decisions** – Delegate down if possible – who is responsible, Decide Now, Gain More Input, Will it work out. Leaders decide on the "what" and empower others to decide on the "how."
- **Get Better Every Time** – Look back – learn from mistakes. Look inward – Condition your mind for decisiveness, Look to the Future – See ahead, Look around – consider a contrarian view.

Die to self in order to hear from the Lord.

> "When God would have us die to self, he always touches the tenderest spot."
>
> —Francois Fenelon

Product

Godly decisions have outcome. He will help us grow spiritually and develop us with contentment and humility to keep us balanced in our faith, which results in greater maturity and wisdom.

The outcome of godly decisions is humility that serves and builds up others, resulting in harmony, respect, and peace.

> "Bless those who persecute you; bless and do not curse. Rejoice with those who rejoice, and weep with those who weep. Be of the same mind toward one another; do not be haughty in mind, but associate with the lowly. Do not be wise in your own estimation. Never repay evil for evil to anyone. Respect what is right in the sight of all people. If possible, so far as it depends on you, be at peace with all people" (Romans 12:14-18).

Growth in our walk of faith

This is a process that takes time and a perspective that is acted upon by faith.

Character

As we grow in making godly decisions our innermost being develops godly character. This character is produced by Christ transforming our hearts and our minds as we give up control and allow him to rule and reign in our life. It is the choosing to surrender that produces humility and this development of character. The Lord is always working to bring us to a point where He has control and He can use us as He wills. The result of this process in the inner man is thankfulness and an outward serving of others. Character often comes through going through trials and difficulty that the Lord uses to form us and to shape us into His will. James 1:2-4 says to *"Consider it all joy, my brethren, when you encounter various trials, knowing that the testing of your faith produces endurance. And let endurance have its perfect result, so that you may be perfect and complete, lacking in nothing."* The goal of character development is maturity that we exercise wisdom and good judgment as we walk with the Lord.

Flexible

As we grow with the Lord we also need to be flexible and to change, because life is full of challenges and opportunities. This flexibility doesn't come from us trying to meet our needs and our desires; it's being sensitive to the leading of the Spirit. if He says to go to the left or to the right, I need to be walking closely enough that I can shift gears and follow Him. Flexibility requires change. We do not change ourselves for the sake of change, but we change as we grow in our vision and our execution and our sensitivity to the needs that are before us. In this change we are called to grow where we are, to live in reality, and not to fantasize about getting our needs met our way.

Maturity owns nothing and gives it all to the Lord.

> **"Maturity is when you live your life by your commitments, not by your feelings."**
>
> **—Rick Warren**

Relationships

In making decisions we must put others ahead of our self-oriented desires. We are called to love others and not our self. We can only do this when we are secure and satisfied.

Consider the following verses that keep things in the right perspective and help us make good decisions.

> *Since you are precious and honored in my sight, and because I love you, I will give people in exchange for you, nations in exchange for your life...everyone who is called by my name, whom I created for my glory, whom I formed and made"* Isaiah 43:4, 7).
>
> *"For the equipping of the saints for the work of ministry, for the building up of the body of Christ; until we all attain to the unity of the faith, and of the knowledge of the Son of God, to a mature man, to the measure of the stature which belongs to the fullness of Christ"* (Ephesians 4:12-13).

In order to make sound decisions in connection with people, let's briefly consider several elements.

Build up the Body

As we make decisions, we need to consider others as more important than ourselves. This is called building up the body, which is noted in first Corinthians 12. The church is the body of Christ, made up of many parts. There are arms, there are legs, there are hands, there are feet. None of us have all of the parts. We serve different roles, and we need one another. So, when we say that we need to build up the body, we build up others, because it's building ourselves. Otherwise, we would be cutting off our hands in our feet for selfish gain.

Help in Conflict Resolution

A key aspect in making decisions is not to be selfish. Selfishness always leads to conflict and division. We are called to resolve conflicts by listening, asking good questions, and then considering the other person's point of view. We can only resolve conflict when we have a love for somebody else, and we put them ahead of our needs and desires. The Lord is honored and loves to see unity. The Bible says that when we walk in unity this will be one of the greatest ways that the world will know that Christ is Lord.

Relationships Help in Decision-making

It takes good relationships to make good decisions. As we've said, we need to put others ahead of ourselves, and this means valuing the relationship and valuing the person in order that there would be unity. But unity doesn't mean that everybody thinks the same and we all look the same. There is a diversity in that unity. But if we approach valuing relationships in our decision-making, then we will take the time to listen and consider another's point of view. There may be a story behind the story that we need to consider. But it always honors the Lord when we lift up others and build up others and hold relationships as more important than our selfish gain.

Another set of eyes

In making decisions we also need to see from another's point of view. This is called getting counsel. That counsel can come from friends or family members or a spouse, but counsel always is helpful to make better decisions. Other people will bring their experiences and their understanding and their wisdom to the situation. So, the sum of the parts is more valuable than any individual part alone. But we need to ask, and we need to listen. The challenge is that often we will seek counsel that goes along with our way of thinking. This "fishing for counsel" is not biblical nor is it wise.

Decide Together – One Another

The Bible give many different imperatives that call us to "one another." We're called to love one another, to serve one another, to care for one another, to lift up one another, to rejoice with one another, and the list goes on. The Lord values the "one another" (the body) as much as He does each individual.

Only two things last—God's Word and people. Give your life to what lasts.

"To love at all is to be vulnerable. Love anything and your heart will be wrung and possibly broken. If you want to make sure of keeping it intact you must give it to no one, not even an *animal. Wrap it carefully round with hobbies and little luxuries; avoid all entanglements. Lock it up safe in the casket or coffin of your selfishness. But in that casket, safe, dark, motionless, airless, it will change. It will not be broken; it will become unbreakable, impenetrable, irredeemable. To love is to be vulnerable."*

—C. S. Lewis

Kingdom Impact

A godly perspective fulfills our purpose and changes the world. We join the Lord in His purposes and see Him bring Kingdom impact through our faithfulness. Keep seeking and expanding the Kingdom. Maintain a healthy fear of God.

As we noted, healthy relationships bring about a Kingdom impact. We are called to have this Kingdom mindset in order to live an eternal life now and forever. One way to do this is to see the impact of our lives beyond our physical years; to have a 200-year horizon. What will be the influence and the impact and product of our life 200 years from now? It will be in the people that we have left behind, how we've influenced them, and the resources that we have given to people. This helps us make better decisions, because we are thinking more than just the day and more than just our own personal lives. This comes from having a clear hope of the future. It has been said that those who have done the most for this world are those who thought about heaven most. Consider the following verses about having an eternal and Kingdom perspective.

"But seek first His kingdom and His righteousness, and all these things will be provided to you" (Matthew 6:33).

"Again, the kingdom of heaven is like a merchant seeking fine pearls, and upon finding one pearl of great value, he went and sold everything that he had and bought it" (Matthew 13:45-46).

Purpose

Having a clear purpose will provide many great benefits. First of all it gives us hope and motivation. It will also lead us to a life of joy contentment peace and security because we are focused and doing what God tells us to do. Having a purpose will give us a true sense of significance and satisfaction, and we will bear much fruit such that at the end of my life, I will hear well done good and faithful servant. A lack of purpose leads to frustration because there are no clear priorities, a life of discontentment. We will start things and not finish them. We will change directions, always seeking the new shiny object.

When we seek to discover our purpose, we should consider the words of Paul: *"For we are His workmanship, created in Christ Jesus for good works, which God prepared beforehand so that we would walk in them"* (Ephesians 2:10). This first tells us that God has a plan and a purpose, and we fit into it. He then gives us a new identity in Him as He calls us to join Him in what He is doing. He then helps us to faithfully carry that out.

Consider the following quotes:

> *"I have concluded that the accumulation of wealth, even if I could achieve it, is an insufficient reason for living. When I reach the end of my days, a moment or two from now, I must look backward on something more meaningful than the pursuit of houses, land, machines, stocks and bonds. Nor is fame any lasting benefit. I will consider my earthly existence to have been wasted unless I can recall a loving family, a consistent investment in the lives of people and an earnest attempt to serve the God who made me. Nothing else makes much sense."*
> —James Dobson, Jr.

> *"In back of every wasted life is a bad philosophy, an erroneous conception of life's worth and purpose. The man who believes that he was born to get all he can will spend his life*

trying to get it. The man who believes he was created to enjoy fleshly pleasures will devote himself to pleasure seeking; and if by a combination of favorable circumstance he manages to get a lot of fun out of life, his pleasures will all turn to ashes in his mouth at the last. He will find out too late that God made him too noble to be satisfied with those tawdry pleasures he had devoted his life to here under the sun."

—A. W. Tozer

Now What?

"Each one must do just as he has decided in his heart, not reluctantly or under compulsion, for God loves a cheerful giver" (2 Corinthians 9:7).

"That He would grant you, according to the riches of His glory, to be strengthened with power through His Spirit in the inner self, so that Christ may dwell in your hearts through faith; and that you, being rooted and grounded in love, may be able to comprehend with all the saints what is the width and length and height and depth, and to know the love of Christ which surpasses knowledge, that you may be filled to all the fullness of God" (Ephesians 3:16-19).

In order to decide well, one must choose using a proven process: Decide. Follow. Step out in Faith. Pursue your Calling. These steps build upon one another and continually work together in the trust of this truth:

- **God sees the future, and I don't. God knows best, and I just think I do.**
- **God loves me and the people in my life more than I ever can.**

> **OBSERVATIONS:** *We all have the opportunity to choose—every moment, every day. We don't control the amount of time of our lives—long or short. We do control our choices of what we do with that time, whether good or bad. Choose humility, and the Lord's grace will be given to you in greater measure. Better to be neutral and listening than sure and talking about your plans and your future.*

Right decisions come from a good process and result in fruit and development in key areas.

- **Understand the will of God** (as outlined previously).
  - » Consult your Friend Jesus. Intimacy and quiet with the Lord.
  - » Gather the facts. Pray, read, gain counsel.
  - » Watch for circumstances. Keep your eyes open.
  - » Get neutral. Decide to surrender, die to self, trust the Lord with the outcome (7 Choices).
- **Seek a character of humility**—fundamental to maturity, exercising wisdom. Not full of self.
  - » Increase your size of the Lord.
- **Listen and hear the Lord.** Be led by the Spirit.
- **Consider your choices.**
- **Give yourself to building others** spiritually and serving others
- **Define your purpose** and write in out.
- **Heart—Commit—Be all in—no reservations.** Don't hold back.

Chapter 4 (e)

ACT INTENTIONALLY

"Start Paddling"

"Take the first step in faith. You don't have to see the whole staircase; just take the first step."
—Martin Luther King, Jr.

Perspective is always reflected in our actions. We need to put our boats in the water and start paddling; we can't progress standing on the shore. We move from **Knowing** to **Being** to **Doing**. The Christian life involves faith, and faith always ends up in action, which is to take a step. The key is that action must be rooted and grounded in the Lord and not in our own strength, desires, mission, or capabilities. It must be directed toward the Lord, the Word, and the Kingdom. Our actions will reflect our beliefs and our following through on what the Lord tells us to do.

Reflect on the following verses that call us to action.

> *"The people who know their God display strength, and take action"* (Daniel 11:32).
>
> *"Therefore, prepare your minds for action, keep sober in spirit, set your hope completely on the grace to be brought to you at the revelation of Jesus Christ"* (1 Peter 1:13).
>
> *"And everyone who hears these words of Mine, and does not act on them, will be like a foolish man who built his house on the sand"* (Matthew 7:26).

"Be on the alert, stand firm in the faith, act like men, be strong" (1 Corinthians 16:19).

As we progress to action, we will look at the action in four ways:

The Activity	The Principles	
Step Out. Grow as You Go.	Process or Product.	FAITH
Walk in the Present.	Be all There – Wholehearted. (Being vs. Doing)	HOPE
Enjoy the Journey.	Thankfulness Satisfies. (Gratitude, Contentment)	LOVE
Excel in Order to Glorify.	Make It Your Purpose to Glorify.	GRACE

Step Out and Grow as You Go

A. Step by Step

Following the Spirit

Be deliberate in your stepping out; don't be reactive and driven. Let the Spirit guide your actions of faith. We are reminded about taking one step at a time: *"Your Word is a lamp to my feet and a light to my path"* (Psalm 119:105). Once we have taken one step, we take another step.

Don't get ahead of yourself or the Lord. Too often, we want the Lord to approve our plans. We must be very careful to be neutral and willing to wait for the Lord's revelation.

Remember that we are in a process of gradual conformity to the image of Christ, so that we can love and serve others along the way. **Sanctification is both an event and a process.**

The Next, Right, Wise Step

Once you've exercised faith to take one step, what do we do? it's important that the steps have direction and purpose. The phrase **"take the next, right, wise step"** is a good way to remember that is not only taking a step, it is taking the "next" step. Then taking the "right" steps, and finally being "wise" in the steps that we take.

B. The Process Is the End

The following devotional by Oswald Chambers helps us understand that we are in a process of growth and that process from God's perspective is the end. It's not that we enter into a process to get somewhere; God wants us to be open as He is at work.

> *"And straightway He constrained His disciples to get into the ship, and to go to the other side..." (Mark 6:45-52).*
>
> *We are apt to imagine that if Jesus Christ constrains us, and we obey Him, He will lead us to great success. We must never put our dreams of success as God's purpose for us; His purpose may be exactly the opposite. We have an idea that God is leading us to a particular end, a desired goal; He is not. The question of getting to a particular end is a mere incident. What we call the process, God calls the end.*
>
> *What is my dream of God's purpose? His purpose is that I depend on Him and on His power now. If I can stay in the middle of the turmoil calm and unperplexed, that is the end of the purpose of God. God is not working towards a particular finish; His end is the process—that I see Him walking on the waves, no shore in sight, no success, no goal, just the absolute certainty that it is all right because I see Him walking on the sea. It is the process, not the end, which is glorifying to God... What men call training and preparation, God calls the end...if we realize that obedience is the end, then each moment as it comes is precious.*

C. Trust – Dependence / Faith

Faith is not an emotion, it is an action of trust. *"Now faith is the certainty of things hoped for, a proof of things not seen...And without faith it is impossible to please Him, for the one who comes to God must believe that*

He exists, and that He proves to be One who rewards those who seek Him" (Hebrews 11:1, 6).

Faith is pleasing to God because it is the measure of the risk we place in His character and promises. Those who trust in Christ are, in effect, "betting the farm" on His claims and credentials; they are hoping that what He has promised, He is able also to perform (Romans 4:21). The essence of walking in faith is acting on the conviction that God alone knows what is best for us and that He alone is able to accomplish it. The problem with faith is that it goes against the grain of human inclination and culture because it is based on the invisible and uncontrollable.

> "A real Christian is an odd number, anyway. He feels supreme love for One whom he has never seen; talks familiarly every day to Someone he cannot see; expects to go to heaven on the virtue of Another; empties himself in order to be full; admits he is wrong so he can be declared right; goes down in order to get up; is strongest when he is weakest; richest when he is poorest and happiest when he feels the worst. He dies so he can live; forsakes in order to have; gives away so he can keep; sees the invisible; hears the inaudible; and knows that which passes knowledge."
>
> —A. W. Tozer

This faith that pleases God involves three components: knowledge, trust, and action.

Component 1: Knowledge. *Unless we know the truth, the truth cannot set us free. Faith in the biblical sense is not based on our feelings and opinions or on those of others, but on the authority of divine revelation. Since the heart cannot rejoice in what the mind rejects, it is important to understand that biblical faith is not a leap into the dark but a step into the light.*

Component 2: Trust. *Faith is only as good as the object in which it is placed. If the object is worthy of our faith, it will sustain us even when our* *faith is weak. There is no more trustworthy foundation for our faith than Christ, the Rock and Anchor of our soul. When we place our trust in Him, we know that He will carry us safely home.*

Component 3: Action. *Knowledge and trust are best displayed in action. Regardless of what we say, it is what we do that will reveal what our hearts truly believe and trust. Faith in Christ has the property of growing through acts of obedience, and an obedient faith results in a greater knowledge of God.*

It is only when we empty our hands of self-reliance, self-righteousness, self-pity, and other self-sins that they will be empty enough to receive the life of Christ in us and display His life to others.

D. Growing and Maturing

Growth in Christian virtues such as obedience, patience, courage, wisdom, service, humility, gentleness, and love is never automatic or easy. This requires a lengthy series of deaths along the way: *"If anyone wishes to come after Me, he must deny himself, and take up his cross and follow Me. For whoever wishes to save his life will lose it, but whoever loses his life for My sake and the gospel's will save it"* (Mark 8:34-35).

Our task is to place ourselves under the conditions favorable to growth and look to God for our spiritual formation. He uses different paces and methods with each person, since the inner life matures and becomes fruitful by the principle of growth and time is a significant part of the process. (See 1 Peter 2:2; 2 Peter 3:18.)

As nature teaches us, growth is not uniform—like a vine or a tree, there may be more growth in a single month than there can be in the other eleven months. **God's timing will seem painfully slow to us, but as we grow in wisdom, we learn to be more patient with the divine process, knowing that He alone knows what we need and when we need it.**

In a culture that promotes instant gratification, it can be wearisome for us to wait patiently for God's timing. Many of us are tempted to bypass grace and take matters into our own hands as we seek some method, technique, seminar, or experience that will give us the results we want when we want them. But the fact is that we are as incapable of changing ourselves through our own efforts as we are of manipulating God to transform us more quickly.

Walk in the Present

As we walk with the Lord, we must stay present in our mind. Not be seeking to live in the past or to dream about the future. We must be all there. In addition, we must be all in, fully committed to the journey. In other words, this means being wholehearted in our faith, not timid or committed. As we are walking, we must not try to straddle the fence, trying to go the Lord's way as well as our own. Also in this walking, we must be flexible and willing to change direction as the Lord leads us. This walking in the presence is building on the faith of our step-by-step process which gives us hope. Hope is the great motivator of our walk.

Enjoy the Journey

A. Process

As we are following the Lord and acting out what God wants us to do, we must understand that the journey is a process; it's not an event. It may take time; it does not happen overnight. So, I have to realize that I need to be patient and thoughtful as well as consistent in my actions going forward. When I have a perspective of life in the journey as a process then I can be at rest and at peace even though I don't know what is going to happen next or I don't have a clear picture about the route I'm taking, but I know that the Lord is guiding me.

As we are walking, we must keep in mind that this is a journey. It is step by step, but it is targeted for the long haul also. In this journey we must have a right mindset or attitude. When we have an attitude of thankfulness and gratitude, this makes the journey much more pleasant. It becomes an adventure of showing up and seeing what God is going to do and appreciating it. This thankfulness brings about true satisfaction in our innermost being and a contentment with what we have been given.

The journey can start small and doesn't necessarily have to be all planned out. The key is to do the little things well and build upon that which has been completed. As we travel along, we must be willing to take risks. The journey is not fully mapped out nor will it always be smooth. There will be challenges setbacks and heartaches along the way. We must learn to accept this as part of the process and learn when we fail.

B. Faithfulness to opportunity

A key aspect of understanding our journey is that I need to be faithful to opportunities I can't control circumstances nor can I make things happen. But I need to see the steps in the opportunities in front of me and be faithful to respond to them in a godly manner. This is what the Lord will reward is faithfulness to opportunity. I may not have all the gifts or time or talent but I need to use what the Lord gives me not trying to do something or comparing myself to someone else.

C. Never a Straight Line

I must also understand as I walk on this journey that it is going to be full of twists and turns. It will not be a straight line. So, I have to be flexible; I have to be adaptable and be able to change as the Lord leads me. But when I give up control of trying to make the decisions myself and trying to determine the outcome, it allows me to be in a place of responding to what God has for me.

D. Takes Time

We also noted the journey will take time. It's not an overnight process. Again, it's not an event; it most likely will be that what God calls me to do will not happen instantly. This is a great challenge for us in this world because we like to see things immediately. This is a part of dying to self by surrendering my expectations and my desires or submitting them under what the Lord has for me. This takes time to develop in our character, and it must be cultivated step-by-step in order to listen and follow the Lord.

E. Vision

Every journey has a destination. This destination or vision of the end comes from the Lord. Man does not come up with the vision; it needs to be God inspired and God directed. But a vision gives us many things: it helps us make choices, it helps us determine priorities, and it helps motivate us. So, it's very important to have a clear vision. In Proverbs 29:18 it says, *"Where there is no vision, the people are unrestrained."* In other words, they're running around with their heads cut off. So, vision keeps us focused and keeps us seeking God's priorities first.

F. Guide

To go on a journey and be fruitful in the process, it is best to have a guide. The guide is more than my intellect or my intuition. The guide truly needs to be the Holy Spirit, Christ in us, guiding and directing us. Reflect on the following verse about God's guidance.

> *"You will guide me with Your plan, and afterward receive me to glory. Whom do I have in heaven but You? and with You, I desire nothing on earth. My flesh and my heart may fail, But God is the strength of my heart and my portion forever"* (Psalm 73:24-25).

A final thought in terms of the journey is that we need to be in the game, not cheering from the sidelines or celebrating other people's progress, being somehow stuck or not participating.

Excel in Order to Glorify

As we journey along, we do things with excellence in order to glorify the Lord. This makes even the smallest task important and a fulfillment of our purpose, because it is about honoring the Lord. We are called to pursue excellence as a means of reflecting how God can use us. This attitude toward excellence is that of adding value or helping other people along the way. It says in Matthew 5:16, *"Let your light shine before men in such a way they may see your good works and glorify God who is in heaven."*

Application: Now What?

> *"Therefore, my beloved brothers and sisters, be firm, immovable, always excelling in the work of the Lord, knowing that your labor is not in vain in the Lord"* (1 Corinthians 15:58).

Every action begins with a first step. Here are seven ways to encourage godly steps of faith.

1. **Take steps of faith** when the Lord directs and the way is clear.
   - Take risks and do not live in fear.

2. **Develop patience** in the areas of your struggles or when working with other people.
   - Look at yourself and the log in your eye rather than the specks in others' eyes.

3. **Ask for wisdom** to overcome being double-minded.
   - Pray.
   - Get counsel.

4. **Do the next, best, right, wise thing.**
   - Be excellent in thought, word, and deed.

5. **Continue to act with thankfulness.**

6. **Have an excellent mindset.**

7. **Be centered in prayer.**

ACT INTENTIONALLY

Chapter 4 (f)

LIVE ABUNDANTLY

"Don't Waste Your Life"

"I have come that they may have life, and have it abundantly"
(John 10:10).

> John Piper quoted from Reader's Digest: *"Bob and Penny...*
> *took early retirement from their jobs in the Northeast five years*
> *ago when he was 59 and she was 51. Now they live in Punta*
> *Gorda, Florida, where they cruise on their thirty-foot trawler,*
> *playing softball and collecting shells."*
>
> That's a tragedy. Don't buy it. With all my heart I plead with
> you: don't buy that dream. The American Dream: a nice house,
> a nice car, a nice job, a nice family, a nice retirement, collecting
> shells as the last chapter before you stand before the Creator
> of the universe to give an account of what you did: "Here it is
> Lord—my shell collection! And I've got a nice swing, and look
> at my boat!"
>
> Don't waste your life; don't waste it.

Perspective should be a lifestyle, not just a series of events or actions. As we have progressed, we have moved from seeing, to thinking, to deciding, and then to acting. When we have done this well, we will then have a life that is well lived. As a beginning of a life lived well, consider the following verses.

"Now I want you to know, brothers and sisters, that my circumstances have turned out for the greater progress of the gospel...For to me, to live is Christ, and to die is gain. But if I am to live on in the flesh, this will mean fruitful labor for me; and I do not know which to choose" (Philippians 1:13, 20-21).

"I have come that they may have life, and have it abundantly" (John 10:10).

"I have been crucified with Christ; and it is no longer I who live, but Christ lives in me; and the life which I now live in the flesh I live by faith in the Son of God, who loved me and gave Himself up for me" (Galatians 2:20).

"Very truly I tell you, unless a kernel of wheat falls to the ground and dies, it remains only a single seed. But if it dies, it produces many seeds. Anyone who loves their life will lose it, while anyone who hates their life in this world will keep it for eternal life" (John 12:24-25).

"Whoever does not take up their cross and follow me is not worthy of me. Whoever finds their life will lose it, and whoever loses their life for my sake will find it" (Matthew 10:38-39).

"Instruct them to do good, to be rich in good works, to be generous and ready to share, storing up for themselves the treasure of a good foundation for the future, so that they may take hold of that which is truly life" (1 Timothy 6:18-19).

We will examine a life with a perspective of a life lived well in four ways.

1. **Posture:** Only in humility can we see our true need and how He will meet our need.

2. **Cultivated:** A clear perspective can be developed through focus and discipline. It is a lifestyle, an eternal life now and forever. Perspective is hard to gain and easy to lose.

3. **Perseverance:** Life is a journey with every turn a new look. We press on. Live in community. Don't go alone.

4. **Eternal Life:** Live the eternal life now and forever.

Posture

The key posture we are to have when living an abundant life is humility. Only in humility can we see our need and how God can and will meet our need. Only in humility can we have good relationships and exercise wisdom.

> *"Do nothing from selfishness or empty conceit, but with humility consider one another as more important than yourselves; do not merely look out for your own personal interests, but also for the interests of others"* (Philippians 2:2-4).
>
> *"Subject yourselves to one another in the fear of Christ"* (Ephesians 5:21).
>
> *"But he gives us more grace. That is why Scripture says: "God opposes the proud but shows favor to the humble...Humble yourselves before the Lord, and he will lift you up"* (James 4:6, 10).

- **Live Humbly**
- **Serving others**
- **Clay pots**
- **Growth**
- **Vulnerable**

Live Humbly. To live humbly is the opposite of being prideful. We are to have a proper view of ourselves, not thinking too highly of ourselves, but seeing ourselves the way God sees us. Humility regards others more important than ourselves, yet humility has many great benefits. Humility frees us from ourselves and frees us from expectations of others. When we see ourselves the way God sees us, we note the amount of grace and forgiveness that He has given us, and that it is undeserved. So, on the one hand we're not worthless, yet we are unworthy, and that grace brings us to a place of humility. Humility also helps us see the Lord properly, and thus we can see ourselves properly in light of Him.

Pride cripples our life. It makes us full of ourselves, and we look to ourselves to get our needs met. This is very displeasing to the Lord, and it also turns off other people. Pride distorts reality and is the root of sin going all the way back to the Garden of Eden. Humility is the key to all relationships because it values others more than ourselves.

Serving others. To live well means that we serve others, build up others, and invest in other people. Our life is not about ourselves, it is not to be self-serving. Thus, when we serve other people, we are acting the way Jesus would act and we're helping other people. This brings us together with others and we need them. As we serve other people, we begin to walk in their shoes and see the way they have been either treated or the challenges that they face. This gives us perspective about them and ourselves. Also, when we serve others, it puts us in a place of thankfulness. It provides an opportunity to better other people and we will be better for it. This is the source of true satisfaction and having an abundant life.

Clay pots. When we see ourselves as a clay pot, easily broken and insufficient, this helps us to realize our need for the Lord, and it also brings about a thankfulness for what God has done for us. That allows us to accept our weaknesses, so that in our weakness the power of Christ may dwell. The other thing about being a clay pot is that we don't put ourselves in a place that is over other people. This sense of being weak or having challenges becomes the basis for ministry and helping others.

Growth. A full, abundant life is a life that is continuing to grow. Growth comes by receiving good things that we enjoy, but it also comes through walking in trials and difficulty. We have seen that the Lord grows us in the times of the difficulties (See James 1:2-4.) To be perfect is to mature, to grow up. It's to become what God wants us to become, and we only do that when we depend upon the Lord. And our dependence on the

Lord is found in those places where we need Him.

Vulnerable. Finally, our posture should be both humble and vulnerable. When we talk about vulnerability, is means that we admit our own needs. It is in our vulnerability that we need the Lord, and we see that we need other people. We cannot live this life alone. God said, *"It is not good for the man to be alone"* (Genesis 2:18). So, in our vulnerability it takes real strength and security to admit it. Too often we feel like we will be manipulated or taken advantage of, and so we put up protections and hide our weaknesses.

Cultivated: A clear perspective can be developed through focus and discipline

Perspective must be cultivated and developed. It must be an intentional pursuit and one you will need to sacrifice for in order to gain it.

> *"When Peter saw him, he asked, 'Lord, what about him?' Jesus answered, 'If I want him to remain alive until I return, what is that to you? You must follow me'"* (John 21:21-22 NIV).
>
> *"Whatever you do, work with all your heart, as working for the Lord, not for human masters, since you know that you will receive an inheritance from the Lord as a reward. It is the Lord Christ you are serving"* (Colossians 3:23-24).

- **Pursue the Lord.**
- **Practice Accountability.**
- **Give Generously.**
- **Forgive.**

Pursue the Lord. Cultivating a life of perspective begins by pursuing the Lord. Why? We do this is to live an abundant life with Christ living in and through us. We have the benefits of both forgiveness as well as a life of joy, love, and power. But what do we pursue? We are called to pursue a relationship with Christ, pursue knowing Him through His Word, where we come to understand His will. How do we pursue Him? We are called to play to the audience of One, and this will take focus and discipline.

Practice Accountability. We all have blind spots and don't see ourselves fully. So, we need to approach other people and ask them to hold us accountable by asking questions and digging into our lives to make sure that our thinking and our perspective are on target. One way to do this is to seek out accountability and ask people to check in on you, asking you the tough questions: How are you doing? How is your walk with the Lord progressing? The people that generally end up crashing in the end have no accountability. Ultimately accountability keeps us close to the Lord.

Give Generously. A way to cultivate a heart that is seeking God's perspective is to have a heart of giving generously. Perspective is not about holding on to things and hoarding things. Often, we lose perspective when we try to get our own needs met. We focus on self and don't give. But as we give of time, talent, and treasure, our relationships will grow.

God promises that he who gives generously will be blessed generously. (See Proverbs 11:24-25.) So, the things that we give away, such as love and grace, grow as we give them. But if we try to hold on to those things, they will diminish. Practice giving financially, giving grace, giving compliments, and building up other people with your words. Don't tear them down, don't talk inappropriately about people or behind their back.

Forgive. The fifth way to cultivate perspective is to give and seek forgiveness. We have been forgiven by the Lord, but as we forgive and seek forgiveness of others, issues or divisions or conflicts are resolved, but we can only forgive as we understand how much we have been forgiven. This helps us keep a heart of appreciation and thankfulness to the Lord.

Perseverance: Keep paddling in the river and pressing on.

To live a life of perspective is not an easy task. It will take much perseverance and the power of the Lord living in and through you. Consider the following verses that highlight perseverance.

"Brothers and sisters, I do not consider myself yet to have taken hold of it. But one thing I do: Forgetting what is behind and straining toward what is ahead, I press on toward the goal to win the prize for which God has called me heavenward in Christ Jesus" (Philippians 3:13-14).

"To the one who is victorious, I will give the right to sit with me on my throne, just as I was victorious and sat down with my Father on his throne" (Revelation 3:21).

- The Enemy is coming.
- Press on.
- Mountains and valleys.
- Handling disappointments.
- Waiting is not easy.

The Enemy is coming. We will need perseverance because the enemy, the devil, is seeking to kill steal and destroy each one of us. The devil has great, yet limited power and dominion in this world, he is real, and he is evil. One must never underestimate or deny the presence and the power of the evil one. This enemy will manifest himself in many ways and through people and institutions in order to get us off track or in the ditch.

Press on. Paul says in Philippians, he says he presses on toward the goal for the prize of the upward call of God in Christ Jesus. We too are called to press on, to push through, and to press into challenges and difficulties of life. The Christian life is not a life of ease and comfort and a lack of problems. In fact, it's going to be more challenging than a life without the Lord in many ways. So, we need to have a mindset of not wanting the absence of problems but to ask for wisdom, power, and for the Lord to walk with us through those challenges. Press in and don't give up.

Mountains and valleys. Embrace the Journey through the mountains and Valleys. Each of us are on a journey of growing in our walk with the Lord, being conformed to His image, becoming mature, and giving our lives away. Each of our journeys are very unique and yet have similarities in the hurdles and difficulties that we all will face. In the end we climb the mountains and yet live in the valleys.

The journey is long and arduous, full of difficulties and setbacks as well as progress and triumph. In our climbing the mountains we are called to master them or be skillful enough to flourish in each step along the way. The final victory is to enjoy the Lord and His reward in eternity along with a rich legacy. Romans 8:37, *"No, despite all these things, overwhelming victory is ours through Christ, who loved us."*

Having a picture or map of the journey gives us perspective as well as helps us navigate the ups and downs along the way. With a map we can anticipate what lies ahead so we are not caught unaware. Each journey has the same destination of HOME, which is an eternal life in heaven with the Lord and His saints.

Handling disappointments. Our perseverance will be called on in times of disappointment and difficulty. There will be trials and challenges in life and some painful and some with great loss. The Lord is not unaware of these difficulties and in fact He gives us the Holy Spirit , the spirit of Christ to help us walk through them. The Father knows great loss because He sacrificed Christ for each one of us. But in handling disappointments we need to first keep our eyes on the Lord and to be thankful. Then call upon the Lord to give us comfort either directly or indirectly through people. But it's only in being with the Lord and being in the care and comfort of those around us , our community, that we can walk through these valleys. Sometimes the Lord allows us to go through the difficulties as a way of protecting us as well as growing us. So do not lose sight of the challenges of this life. The Lord may be protecting you as He is growing you.

Waiting is not easy. Having to wait can be necessary and helpful. We need to learn how to wait upon the Lord. Waiting is not easy because we do not know the Lord's time schedule or what the Lord is doing. But the Bible is very clear: Several times it admonishes us to wait on the Lord. The Lord allows us to wait and wants us to wait to produce dependence and humility.

Life Eternal: Perspective is hard to gain and easy to lose.

Keeping perspective that our life is eternal is not an easy task. But the outcome will be one of great blessing. Note as we appropriate Christ, *"God is able to do exceeding abundantly beyond all that we could ask or imagine"* (Ephesians 3:16-21).

- **Easy to lose.**
- **Comfort heals.**
- **Life Together.**
- **Well done, good and faithful servant.**
- **Finish well.**

Easy to lose. Be reminded that living life with an eternal perspective is easy to lose. As we face hindrances or we have blind spots, we take our eyes off the Lord and His work in and through our lives. So, just be careful to realize then it's going to take His strength to work through you, otherwise you will lose perspective quickly. The world wants to distract us, divert us, have us focus on entertainment, blame other people, and not take responsibility for our own actions. This is how we lose perspective.

Comfort heals. Comfort comes from God and Christ. Note the following verses of how we are comforted by the Lord. Comfort does not come from possessions or riches, it comes from the Lord. The Lord brings healing through forgiveness which is a comfort. As we have received comfort, we minister comfort and grace to an area of hurt or loss to others. You minister spirit to spirit and emotion to emotion, not logic to emotion. (See Corinthians 1:3-7; 2 Corinthians 7:6-7.)

Life Together. We are called into relationships with one another as God designed man to need one another in order to relate to God and to function in His purposes. Community meets needs and resolves conflict. We are called to be with one another. Life together is best when we serve, help, and invest in others. When we realize we are not the center of life, we can get beyond our self-importance and value others by serving them. Consider the following scriptural commands.

- Love one another. (See John 13:34-35.)
- Be of the same mind toward one another. (See Romans 12:16.)
- Serve one another. (See Galatians 5:13.)
- Provoke one another to love and good deeds. (See Hebrews 10:24.)
- Be kind to one another. (See Ephesians 4:32.)
- Submit yourselves to one another. (See Ephesians 5:21.)

"I think it's beautiful how God has put the body together. I need my weaknesses as much as I need my strengths because if I didn't have my weaknesses I wouldn't need you. And if I don't have you I'd be so much impoverished for the lack of relationship. So there is real beauty in how it's put together. We should not be down on ourselves because of our weaknesses. We should give thanks for them because it is the glue that holds us together in the body. I should be thankful for what I don't have because this creates a bond that you and I wouldn't have otherwise."

—Jim Petersen

"Nothing is sweet or easy about community. Community is a fellowship of people who do not hide their joys and sorrows but make them visible to each other in a gesture of hope. In community we say: Life is full of gains and losses, joys and sorrows, ups and downs—but we do not have to live it alone. We want to drink our cup together and thus celebrate the truth that the wounds of our individual lives, which seem intolerable when live alone, become sources of healing when we live them as part of a fellowship of mutual care."

—Henri Nouwen

"The elimination of the weak is the death of the fellowship. The exclusion of the weak and insignificant; the seemingly useless people, from a Christian community may actually mean the exclusion of Christ; in the poor brother Christ is knocking at the door."

—Dietrich Bonhoffer

Well done, good and faithful servant. *"Well done, good and faithful slave. You were faithful with a few things, I will put you in charge of many things; enter into the joy of your master"* (Matthew 25:21, 23).

This is the final step and destination of our life on earth. "Well done" literally means "great job, from now on be my partner!" It is a picture of how we are to glorify and be pleasing to the Lord. We are to have excellence in work, be set apart, and finish well. To hear "well done" is our greatest desire. The only way to hear "well done" is through a vibrant relationship with Christ. That is much different than the world's relationships and can be revealed through the paradoxes of the Christian life that are at the heart of our faith.

Being faithful is even more daunting. The word translated as "faithful" means "trustful," "obedient," "loyal," "deserving belief" and "consistent character." It has both the sense of trusting someone else and being trustworthy. So, as we journey in the midst of the world's morass, we are to be trustworthy, counted on, and consistent. Faithful implies both a relationship to the one you report to and to a world who is watching.

Finally, we are called to the role of slave or servant—someone who is helping another. This is the picture of Christ throughout His life and ministry here are earth. We are called to be and do likewise.

Finish well. Kingdom impact should have a perspective of finishing well. Paul said he ran the race in order that he would finish well. What does finishing well look like? Finishing well includes having godly character, putting others ahead of ourselves, investing in Kingdom endeavors, and living so that our life would reflect and honor the Lord. Finishing well is a matter of both obedience and loving Christ as well as others. The greatest honor of finishing well is to hear from Christ: "Well done good and faithful servant; enter into the joy of your master." We can only finish well when we keep the end in mind. If our eyes are on the moment, we will make poor decisions. We need to lift up our eyes and look to the horizons.

There are seven absolutes to living well and finishing strong.

1. Keep **Jesus** and the **Gospel** central in order to live as Christ and seek His eternal Kingdom. Christ is the Christian life lived out through us, and apart from Him we can do nothing. Are we engaged in God's purposes of evangelism and discipleship? Be centered first in Christ (John 15:5) and then be balanced in life.

2. Bring order to our **Money** and **Finances** to lay a foundation for freedom and peace. Without a sense of order, we will be in chaos or consumed by money and our attitudes toward money. Do we have a stewardship perspective?

3. Clarify why you go to **Work** and what your **Purpose** is. This will produce direction and priorities. We are called to work and commanded to provide for the needs of our families. Work is important but should not consume us or define who we are. Work should be a platform where we exhibit and model Christ.

4. Define true **Success** and **Significance** to empower our motivation and refine our motives. To have balance and perspective, a biblical view of success and significance is critical.

5. Value **Relationships** and **Community** with love to create wholeness and give meaning to life. God created this world and people were His highest creation. He made us in His image, and not even angels have this distinction.

6. Respond appropriately to life's **Circumstances** and **Challenges** because it will build or break you. Having a right perspective is critical, or we may focus too much on the losses and become upset with the Lord or frustrated with others.

7. Handle your **Resources** with **Generosity** in order to bless others and reap an eternal reward. Practice contentment. If you are not satisfied with a little, you will not be satisfied with a lot. The Lord gives us many things: finances, talents, gifts, abilities, and relationships, just to name a few. What have we done with what we were given?

> *"But I do not consider my life of any account as dear to myself, so that I may finish my course and the ministry which I received from the Lord Jesus, to testify solemnly of the gospel of the grace of God"* (Acts 20:24).

How we live today impacts eternity.

> *"Death is nothing else but going home to God, the bond of love will be unbroken for all eternity."*
>
> —Mother Teresa

Application

Living with perspective will require pressing in both to the good and to the challenges of life. *"When the perishable has been clothed with the imperishable, and the mortal with immortality, then the saying that is written will come true: 'Death has been swallowed up in victory.'…But thanks be to God! He gives us the victory through our Lord Jesus Christ"* (1 Corinthians 15:54, 57).

1. **Work on your posture of humility.** Ask for others to examine areas of blind spots.

2. **Keep being thankful in all things.**

3. **Exercise and take hold of God's power.**

4. **A clear perspective is an act of cultivation.** Be disciplined in the word and prayer.

5. **Eternal Life: Live the eternal life.** Reflect on eternity and how many years you have to live.

6. **Perseverance: Life is a journey.** Keep pressing on in the areas of trials. Be accountable.

"Therefore, since we are surrounded by such a great cloud of witnesses, let us throw off everything that hinders and the sin that so easily entangles. And let us run with perseverance the race marked out for us, fixing our eyes on Jesus, the pioneer and perfecter of faith. For the joy set before him he endured the cross, scorning its shame, and sat down at the right hand of the throne of God" (Hebrews 12:1-2).

"Blessed be the God and Father of our Lord Jesus Christ, the Father of mercies and God of all comfort, who comforts us in all our affliction so that we will be able to comfort those who are in any affliction with the comfort with which we ourselves are comforted by God. For just as the sufferings of Christ are ours in abundance, so also our comfort is abundant through Christ" (2 Corinthians 1:3-7).

"But God, who comforts the depressed, comforted us by the coming of Titus; and not only by his coming, but also by the comfort with which he was comforted in you, as he reported to us your longing, your mourning, your zeal for me; so that I rejoiced even more" (2 Corinthians 7:6-7).

"That He would grant you, according to the riches of His glory, to be strengthened with power through His Spirit in the inner self, so that Christ may dwell in your hearts through faith; and that you, being rooted and grounded in love, may be able to comprehend with all the saints what is the width and length and height and depth, and to know the love of Christ which surpasses knowledge, that you may be filled to all the fullness of God" (Ephesians 3:16-21).

Consider the forces and conditions that exist on every mountain and in every valley in our lives.

1. God is on the throne and in control. He is good and always has our best interests at heart. Christ is our hope.

2. Age does not dictate or influence if we grow and progress in our journey. Knowing where you have been directs your path forward and encourages you in the progress you have made.

3. We live in evil days. Life will always have challenges. The Lord doesn't remove them, He walks us through them.

4. Satan is alive and on the warpath against us. He is always seeking to kill, steal, and destroy.

5. We have it all. Every believer has "the gift" of Christ—**intimacy** marked by the unconditional love from God, our **identity** which is being a new person "in Christ," and the **indwelling** of the Holy Spirit.

6. We are all called to seek God's will and Kingdom. The journey is one of growing in His Kingdom on earth. Out of receiving God's love we should desire to obey, walk in faith, and exercise the disciplines. We choose.

7. We need one another (community) in order to progress. We will never survive going alone.

8. We all will be held accountable for our life and be given a reward for our deeds on earth, good or bad.

9. We can be at several places at the same time: i.e., chaos in finances and maturity in relationships.

10. You can move forward and backward in the journey. We do have an enemy who is continually pushing us back.

Only the secure can be humble.

"These are the few ways we can practice humility:
To speak as little as possible of one's self.
To mind one's own business.
Not to want to manage other people's affairs.
To accept contradictions and correction cheerfully.

> *To pass over the mistakes of others.*
> *To accept insults and injuries.*
> *To accept being slighted, forgotten and disliked.*
> *To be kind and gentle even under provocation.*
> *Never to stand on one's dignity.*
> *To choose always the hardest."*
>
> —Mother Teresa

Reflections

- Christ is your life and the hope of your calling. Go into the world and make disciples. We change and grow by going.

- Be others-centered and invest in relationships. Mentor, serve, and always add value to others. Leave a legacy. (See 2 Timothy 2:1-2.)

- Give generously. Be a steward in your lifestyle. Be debt-free. Learn contentment. Things distract you from God's purpose.

- Life is not about us. It is all about giving yourself away. Be relevant in the culture where you live. Bring hope to a dark world.

- Don't go alone. We need people. Value and respect others. Recognize your strengths and weaknesses.

- Give away your strengths, and embrace your weaknesses. Be vulnerable. Lift up others in their burdens.

- Being real and vulnerable; it actually attracts good people.

- Life will be full of challenges and setbacks, don't be discouraged and keep walking through the valleys.

A final reflection about eternity is found in the wisdom and yet emptiness of Steve Jobs' final words. He clearly sees that money, power, position, and possessions don't fulfill, yet his sense of true happiness ultimately does not fulfill either.

A billionaire, Jobs died at 56 years of age of pancreatic cancer. Here are his last words from his sick bed:

"I reached the pinnacle of success in the business world. In others' eyes my life is an epitome of success. However, aside from work, I have little joy. In the end, wealth is only a fact of life that I am accustomed to. At this moment, lying on the sick bed and recalling my whole life, I realize that all the recognition and wealth that I took so much pride in, have paled and become meaningless in the face of impending death.

You can employ someone to drive the car for you, make money for you, but you cannot have someone to bear the sickness for you.

Material things lost can be found. But there is one thing that can never be found when it is lost—'Life.'

As we grow older, and hence wiser, we slowly realize that—
- Wearing a $300 or $30 watch—they both tell the same time...
- Whether we carry a $300 or $30 wallet/handbag—the amount of money inside is the same;
- Whether we drive a $150,000 car or a $30,000 car, the road and distance is the same, and we get to the same destination;
- Whether we drink a bottle of $300 or $10 wine—the hangover is the same;
- Whether the house we live in is 300 or 3000 sq. ft.—loneliness is the same.

You will realize, your true inner happiness does not come from the material things of this world.

Whether you fly first or economy class, if the plane goes down—you go down with it...

Therefore...I hope you realize, when you have mates, buddies and old friends, brothers and sisters, who you chat with, laugh with, talk with, sing songs with, talk about north-south-east-west or heaven and earth...That is true happiness!"

(https://medium.com/@vikasjangir/steve-jobs-last-words-d79012fad236)

Chapter 5

NAVIGATING THE POSSIBILITY PATH

"You've got to be very careful if you don't know where you are going, because you might not get there."
—Yogi Berra

"If you don't know where you are going, any road will get you there."
—Lewis Carroll

"Knowing where you are going is the first step to getting there."
—Ken Blanchard

Perspective is fueled by our questions, which guide our decisions. How we engage life will direct our steps and our relationships.

The Power of Perspective helps you look at life differently, consider eternity among the temporal chaos, and take strong stands and actions leading us to live abundantly in a world of self, suffering, and evil. This can only be done by exercising godly wisdom centered in Christ and then rightly applying it to life and Its challenges. Gaining wisdom when the world has lost it will set us apart. It is not easy, yet it is the only means of life.

> *"That your faith would not rest on the wisdom of men, but on the power of God"* (1 Corinthians 2:5).

Possibility Path

We have just taken a deep dive into five ways we can gain perspective and live life differently. Once we have this new view, we must move forward on the path the Lord has set out for us. I call this the "possibility path" because with the Lord, all things are possible. This promise is repeated five times in three of the gospels. These verses give us much hope.

> *"And looking at them, Jesus said to them, 'With people this is impossible, but with God all things are possible'"* (Matthew 19:26).
>
> *"But Jesus said to him, 'If You can? All things are possible for the one who believes'"* (Mark 9:23).
>
> *"Looking at them, Jesus said, 'With people, it is impossible, but not with God; for all things are possible with God'"* (Mark 10:27).
>
> *"And He was saying, 'Abba! Father! All things are possible for You; remove this cup from Me; yet not what I will, but what You will'"* (Mark 14:36).
>
> *"But He said, 'The things that are impossible with people are possible with God'"* (Luke 18:27).

As we walk by faith in life, our future possibilities are multiple, yet it does not mean one can do anything they want or desire, the key is our alignment with the Lord. This alignment is influenced by three factors.

1. **Our Mindset**
2. **Our Listening**
3. **Our Stepping Out in Faith**

Our Mindset

A mindset is a frame of reference by which we process circumstances, make decisions, and take action. To gain God's view of the possibilities, it is imperative that we ask ourselves eight questions so we are looking in the right direction and able to consider the opportunities. These questions set the stage, lead us, and shape us. They are a filter system by which we explore and discover the open doors of possibility.

Curious or Critical? A curious mindset looks at a situation and believes there are multiple ways to go forward. Curiosity takes discipline and a certain amount of creativity to think beyond what is right in front of us. A critical mindset sees all of the negatives of the opportunities and dismisses them before any action can be taken. Curiosity attracts ideas and people, where a critical spirit repels ideas in people.

Accepting or Judging? An accepting mindset believes the best about opportunities and approaches them with a positive viewpoint. An accepting mindset, as it relates to people, views the best about people and seeks to build them up offering grace in the process. A judging mindset comes to conclusions prematurely and discounts opportunities because there may be uncertainty associated with them. A judging mindset in relation to people puts them down or negatively views them.

Thankful or Dissatisfied? A thankful mindset sees the good in every circumstance and appreciates how the Lord might be working and how good He is in every situation. Gratefulness can color our world in profound ways. If we are dissatisfied, we discount the good things and see essentially what is not in the cup. We essentially are trying to get our needs met our way.

Seek to Serve or Be Served? Our mindset should be one of seeking to serve others and help others grow and not be focused on ourselves. By serving them we keep our eyes off what we have or don't have. Yet if our mindset is to be served or that we need to be first ahead of others, it promotes selfishness and diminishes our spirit.

Focused on the Present or Past/Future? One must keep a mindset of living in the moment or being present well in every situation. Too often we can be either stuck in the past and our memories, good or bad, or we can be dreaming and thinking about the future and not be aware of our current circumstances.

Faith or Fear? A mindset of faith sees possibilities, and even if there are uncertainties or unknowns, there is a willingness to move forward. A fearful mindset generally takes no action and misses out on the possibilities that the Lord has for us. The Lord does not give us the spirit of fear, but it comes from both the enemy and a too large reliance upon our emotions.

Abundance or Poverty? We must approach life with an abundance mentality; in other words, the only limiting factor in life is the Lord and not just what we see. But if we see life from a poverty mentality or a scarcity mindset, then we're going to always seek to serve ourselves first, or we'll hold on to things and not be willing to take risks. The poverty mindset perpetuates a sense of emptiness and despair. An abundance mindset is filled with hope and opportunity. Full or empty.

Connected or Alone? The final mindset is not to try to go alone or market things in our strength. Rather, it is to go together with people. When we live life in community, we are much richer for it, and we enjoy the ups and downs and can persevere through the difficulties much easier. Live in community or live isolated.

So, as we start down the possibility path, we have to set our minds upon the right answers to these eight questions. This sets us up to be able to consider almost an infinite number of possibilities. Be careful not to limit yourselves to the idea of a single solution or path forward.

Our Listening

Once we gain the right mindset by walking through these eight questions, we are now ready to listen and hear from the Lord. It's not only what we want or feel like we need, but it is aligning ourselves in a way that God can reveal the path forward for us. To listen to the Lord takes becoming still and putting out of our mind the distractions and the busyness of all the things going on around us. This discipline to listen starts with rest and empties our minds of our self while at the same time asking the Lord to reveal His ways forward. This is a means both of prayer and reflection upon God's Word, because these are the primary means upon which God reveals His direction and His will.

In this listening process, get alone with God and take a blank piece of paper and say nothing, but listen in your spirit to what is God saying or revealing to you. This may take some time, and there are also times when the Lord says wait and He doesn't reveal things. In these times we need to be thankful and restful and trust the Lord that He is not playing games with us but truly wants our best and will reveal His path forward.

Our Stepping Out in Faith

As the Lord reveals His direction and way forward for us, we must exercise faith to step out and take action. Faith does not overanalyze or try to get everything all lined up before we take action. Faith is known as risk-taking or commitment before a full 100% clarity. But the faith is based upon God's best for our and our belief in Him that He is guiding and directing our path.

When we step out in faith, we must be prepared to enter into the adventure of the unknown. We need to keep our faith grounded or the enemy will come in and steal the joy or fill us with fear.

Observations and Promises

As we consider and proceed down this path of possibility, we need to keep in mind the following promises:

- The Lord has our best interests at heart. This is based on His love, sacrifice, and His nature. It is personal and relational.

- God is in control of both the process and the outcome. The Lord knows all things, knows the future, knows both good and bad.

- He is approachable and wants to answer our prayer.

- God stands beyond time and space, so He has wisdom that is infinite.

- God loves us unconditionally and infinitely.

- There's nothing we can do to stop this; nothing we can do to earn this. It's on the basis of Christ and His grace.

- The Lord uses all things for good, especially the difficulties, to mold shape and correct us.

- The Lord wins in the end; He has power and will defeat the enemy.

- The Lord's character and nature is our foundation and our hope. We can depend upon it.

- God will bring His promises to pass.

- The Lord is with us; He will never leave us nor forsake us.

- With the Lord's perspective directing and guiding us, we are given the opportunity to embrace the magnificent promises of God.

Chapter 6

PLAYING THE LONG GAME IN THE MOMENT

"The temporal and eternal perspectives are competing paradigms of life. We can live as if this world is all there is or we can view our earthly existence as a brief pilgrimage designed to prepare us for eternity. The men and women in Hebrews 11 embraced the latter perspective: 'All these died in faith, without receiving the promises, but having seen them and having welcomed them from a distance and having confessed that they were strangers and exiles on the earth' (Hebrews 11:13). By contrast, those who adopt a temporal paradigm treat the temporal as though it were eternal and the eternal as though it were temporal."

—Ken Boa

We are Living an Eternal Life in the Midst of a World of Darkness and Despair

The "Long Game" is the eternal future, and the "Moment" is the temporal now. Both are important, real, and to be engaged in at the same time. We live this life in a world that is influenced by evil, filled with darkness, and offers no lasting hope. Thus, we need our hearts, eyes, and minds open to be able to navigate, be fruitful, and finish well in this life, prepared for an eternity with Christ.

To play the "long game" takes four things: a clear purpose, proper personal attitudes, others-centeredness, and embracing the promises of God, all of which are encouraging and help us set our expectation.

A Clear Purpose

- The long game mindset is rooted in purpose and values and is our source of hope.
- The long game clarifies true priorities to better live in the moment.
- The long game serves a just cause that is good for everyone.
- The long game is about finishing well.
- The outcome of the long game perspective yields peace, multiplying fruit, eternal rewards, joy, and hope.
- The long game is full of uncertainties, ups, and downs, with no clear path forward.

Proper Personal Attitudes

- Thankfulness and dependence on the Lord is the foundation for the long game.
- Long game choices are intentional, less emotional, and proactive.
- The long game mindset will shape us and will change our moments; it is played with grit and perseverance.
- The long game perspective takes attitudes that include faith, patience, hope, and love.
- The actions of the long game are deliberate, innovative, collaborative, and focused.
- A long game perspective is about continual improvement, aiming toward excellence (being your best).
- With a long game mindset, one is more resilient and presses on through difficulties and setbacks.
- The long game perspective is founded on wisdom from the Lord.
- The long game is still only lived a day at a time.

Others-Centeredness

- The long game is others-centered and best done in a safe, trusting team environment.
- The requirements of the long game are faith, interdependence on people, purpose, and flexibility.
- A long game mindset requires trust and vulnerability and is best in a team environment.

Embracing the Promises of God

- **He gives strength and rest to the weary.** *"But those who hope in the Lord will renew their strength. They will soar on wings like eagles; they will run and not grow weary, they will walk and not be faint"* (Isaiah 40:31). *"Come to me, all who labor and are heavy laden, and I will give you rest. Take my yoke upon you, and learn from me, for I am gentle and lowly in heart, and you will find rest for your souls. For my yoke is easy, and my burden is light"* (Matthew 11:28-30).

- **His love never fails.** *"For the mountains may depart and the hills be removed, but my steadfast love shall not depart from you"* (Isaiah 54:10).

- **He has redeemed and adopted you.** *"He has delivered us from the domain of darkness and transferred us to the kingdom of his beloved Son, in whom we have redemption, the forgiveness of sins"* (Colossians 1:13-14). *"He predestined us for adoption to himself as sons through Jesus Christ, according to the purpose of his will"* (Ephesians 1:5).

- **The Lord will fight for you, and the enemy flee from you.** *"Fear not, stand firm, and see the salvation of the Lord, which he will work for you today. For the Egyptians whom you see today, you shall never see again. The Lord will fight for you, and you have only to be silent"* (Exodus 14:13, 14). *"Submit yourselves therefore to God. Resist the devil, and he will flee from you"* (James 4:7).

- **God gives wisdom to those who ask.** *"If any of you lacks wisdom, let him ask God, who gives generously to all without reproach, and it will be given him"* (James 1:5).

- **He forgives us when we confess our sins.** *"If we confess our sins, he is faithful and just to forgive us our sins and to cleanse us from all unrighteousness"* (1 John 1:9).

- **He will exalt the humble.** *"Whoever exalts himself will be humbled, and whoever humbles himself will be exalted"* (Matthew 23:12).

- **He will never leave or forsake you.** *"Be strong and courageous. Do not fear or be in dread of them, for it is the Lord your God who goes with you. He will not leave you or forsake you"* (Deuteronomy 31:6).

- **He has given us eternal life.** *"For God so loved the world, that he gave his only Son, that whoever believes in him should not perish but have eternal life"* (John 3:16).

- **He will meet all your needs and give you the desires of your heart.** *"And my God will supply every need of yours according to his riches in glory in Christ Jesus"* (Philippians 4:19). *"Delight yourself in the Lord, and he will give you the desires of your heart"* (Psalm 37:4).

Living in the moment incorporates possessing a right focus while living in the tension of potential challenges.

A Right Focus
- We can only live in the moment, so make every day count. Be careful not to live in the past or future.
- Life is a process of moment-by-moment steps each day. Practice His presence daily. Enter His rest and peace.
- One needs to be engaged in the moment by being present, focused, and alert.
- Playing the long game in the moment necessitates a bi-focal vision —to see the day and that day.
- The challenges and trials of the moment don't determine the outcome yet can shape and enhance it.
- Be flexible in the moment, keeping your eyes on the eternal.

Potential Challenges
- A moment mindset can be controlling and competitive.
- A moment mindset has finite resources, which we are vying for.
- A moment mindset can be self-oriented, selfish, and self-centered.
- The moment is often about winning versus losing, accumulating, and striving.
- The moment can be emotional, reactive, and quick to change.

- The moment can be more focused on getting ahead, needs, and desires.

The following excerpt on the Temporal and the Eternal comes from Ken Boa in his book *Conformed to His image*. This is used with permission.

The problem is that we have been captured by a temporal paradigm because we live in a temporal arena. It takes great risk to shift to a biblical paradigm, because it challenges everything that our culture reinforces. The more we have invested in the cultural paradigm and the better we are at functioning within it, the more we think we may lose by changing to the biblical paradigm. It is only when we renew our minds with biblical truth and reinforce this truth through relationships with other children of the kingdom that we begin to see that we really are on a very brief pilgrimage indeed. When we see this, we discover that we must pursue the things that will last rather than the things that are passing away. The problem is that this temporal/eternal shift, unlike the Copernican revolution in astronomy, is reversible; we can flip-flop back and forth between these opposing perspectives. This is an ongoing struggle that we can expect to encounter for the remainder of our worldly sojourn.

As we discover the decline of our capacities and the increase of our responsibilities, we realize with clarity and force that we will not be able to fulfill many of our earthly hopes and dreams. This can be traumatic for those whose expectations are limited to this planet, but for believers whose hope is in the character and promises of God, it can be a powerful reminder to transfer their affections and ambitions to their only true home, the kingdom of heaven.

Tozer goes on to add this important thought: "How completely satisfying to turn from our limitations to a God who has none. *Eternal years lie in His heart. For Him time does not pass, it remains; and those who are in Christ share with Him all the riches of limitless time and endless years."*

The responsibilities and pressures of this world clamor for our attention and tend to squeeze out our inner lives and starve our souls. When this happens, we lose sight of the things that really matter and focus on the things that are passing away. Our value systems become confused when we invest more of our thought and concern in things that are doomed to disappear than in that which will endure forever.

Does this mean that we should be so heavenly minded that we are of no earthly good? In actual fact, it is precisely the opposite—when people become heavenly minded, they treasure the passing opportunities of this life and become more alive to the present moment. Rather than being overwhelmed with the problems and hassles of life, they understand that these too will pass, and that "the sufferings of this present time are not worthy to be compared with the glory that is to be revealed to us" (Romans 8:18). Instead of taking things for granted, they learn to savor blessings and joys that are otherwise overlooked.

Since people will go into eternity, our other-centered acts of kindness and sacrificial service that are borne out of the love of Christ will endure forever.

The world raises wealth and status as a standard of success, security, and identity. But as C. S. Lewis noted in The Screwtape Letters, "Prosperity knits a man to the World. He feels that he is 'finding his place in it,' while really it is finding its place in him His increasing reputation, his widening circle of acquaintances, his sense of importance, the growing pressure of absorbing and agreeable work, build up in him a sense of being really at home in earth." The Word elevates the standard of integrity and character. ("But you, are you seeking great things for yourself? Do not seek them" Jeremiah 45:5.) God sometimes grants the severe mercy of taking His children's toys away for a time so that they will transfer their hope from the creation to the Creator.

The world drives us to amass power over people and circumstances; the Word tells us to walk humbly before our God. "Humble yourselves, therefore, under the mighty hand of God, that He may exalt you at the proper time, casting all your anxiety upon Him, because He cares for you" (1 Peter 5:6-7).

Any attempt to pursue both the claims of the temporal and the eternal is like holding onto two horses that are galloping in opposite directions. The simultaneous pursuit of the kingdom of the world and the kingdom of Christ is impossible—at any point, one or the other will prevail. Many have tried to have it both ways, but this can never be more than a matter of adding a thin spiritual veneer over the same furniture that is manufactured and promoted by the world system.

It takes great risk to let loose of everything we have been taught to clamor after and control. It is never comfortable or natural to treasure the invisible over the visible, the promises of God over the promises of the world, the things that will not be fulfilled until the return of Christ over the things the world says we can have here and now. We want control and security on our own terms, yet the Scriptures tell us that the only true security comes from abandoning the illusion of control and surrendering ourselves unreservedly to the Person and purposes of God.

People think they want pleasure, recognition, popularity, status, and power, but the pursuit of these things leads, in the final analysis, to emptiness, delusion, and foolishness. God has set eternity in our hearts (Ecclesiastes 3:11), and our deepest desires are fulfillment (love, joy, peace), reality (that which does

> *not fade away), and wisdom (skill in living). The only path to this true fulfillment lies in the conscious choice of God's value system over that which is offered by this world. This choice is based on trusting a Person we have not yet seen. "And though you have not seen Him, you love Him, and though you do not see Him now, but believe in Him, you greatly rejoice with joy inexpressible and full of glory, obtaining as the outcome of your faith the salvation of your souls" (1 Peter 1:8-9).*

But the crucial contrast lies in where these opposing value systems ultimately lead:

TEMPORAL	ETERNAL
Pleasure	Knowing God
Recognition of People	Approval of God
Popularity	Servanthood
Wealth and Status	Integrity and Character
Power	Humility
↓	↓
Emptiness	Fulfillment
Delusion	Reality
Foolishness	Wisdom

Having an Eternal Mindset Allows Us to Finish Well

"Finishing Well" was discussed in the chapter on "Don't Waste Your Life," so we will just highlight some bullet points for us to keep in mind.

- Our walk with the Lord is a long game obedience in following. It keeps bearing much fruit, yet it can be lost in a moment. (See Colossians 2:6-7.)
- Seek to hear well done, good and faithful servant, enter into the joy of your master. (See Matthew 25.)
- Only with an eternal view can we truly live in the temporal world; it holds no grip on us. We are aliens in exile. (See Philippians 3:20.)

- Give up what you can't keep, to gain what you can't lose. Reward in heaven helps us endure and know life is fleeting. (See Matthew 6:33.)
- The cost of the temporal is nothing compared to the gain of the eternal. (See Matthew 6:19-24.)
- Press on to our eternal home. Stand firm in warfare. (See Philippians 3:20.)
- We are called and should have a desire to finish well. This can only be done in the Lord's strength and will.
- Grit and perseverance can outweigh intelligence, circumstances, or wealth. (See Philippians 3:8, 12, 14.)

Application to Play the Long Game in the Moment

- **Walk Worthy** – Walk by faith in Christ knowing you are significant and He indwells you.
- **Engage the Culture** – face down the enemies, the world, and your flesh.
- **Embrace the Challenges** – step up when times are the toughest.
- **Be Generous with Resources** – lift up the downtrodden.
- **Seek the Eternal Life** – now and forever.
- **Never give up.**

Chapter 7

GO CHANGE THE WORLD

Conclusion: Be the change in a world that is adrift and headed to nowhere without hope.

Our view of life drives how we do life and has an impact beyond ourselves. We are called to be a catalyst for changing lives and be a part of making an eternal difference.

We have been on a journey in our pursuit of the *Power of Perspective.* We have stopped to consider the need for a new outlook and what the benefits could be. We dug deep into the process of finding this perspective through the means of seeing, thinking, choosing, acting, and living out a God-view of life. Having received this viewpoint, we considered how to hear from the Lord as to the possibilities and path going forward. The capstone of perspective is to play the long game at the moment; in other words, to live with an eternal mindset in a temporal world, to be a conduit for God's infinite power to produce an abundance of fruit through you.

Perspective allows us to reflect, grow, and align ourselves with the Lord so we may be His instruments to accomplish His purposes. The world needs hope and people who can be God's agents of change.

Thoughts

1. All that glitters is not gold. All perceived outcomes are not beneficial. All change is not necessarily good.

2. When embracing change, begin with the end in mind. Keep the eternal your focus.

3. Perspectives are more than a positive mental attitude where we think we can do something.

4. Finding perspective is not a guessing game. It's not let's make a deal or best two out of three.

5. Our words have an impact for good or for bad. They influence us as well as others.

6. You can't walk on water if you don't get out of the boat.

7. Life is lived in the moment, but the focus is best when looking beyond.

8. Selfishness distorts a proper perspective. Be willing to examine your heart and call out selfishness.

9. We can easily find ourselves living in a bubble that blinds us to reality.

10. One never truly lives unless he has something to die for; live for a purpose beyond yourself and your time.

11. Everyone dies, not everyone lives. Few people live an abundant life.

12. Pursuing God's perspective opens doors of opportunity unknown to those who are stuck.

13. Different perspectives help to resolve issues and connect us to others.

14. Perspective is being able to see the forest for the trees.

15. Perspective gives us a new identity so we no longer need to fight circumstances or others.

What you look for you will find, and what you pursue you will obtain

Wait on the Lord (see Isaiah 40), redeem the time. Struggles mold and shape us. Dead ends lead to open doors, pain perfects, humbles, connects us to the true Source of life, and connects us to others.

Final Applications

1. **Guard your emotions.**
   - » Don't let your emotions drive you all over the map.
   - » Keeping emotions in check keeps the enemy from making a mess of our situation.

2. **Pray without ceasing.**
   - » This will connect us to the Lord, gain His wisdom, and change us.

3. **Get outside yourself.**
   - » See and think from God's view.
   - » Walk in someone else's shoes; hear their story.

4. **Let go of trying to control what you can't.**
   - » Control is a product of fear, insecurity, and/or pride.
   - » Control what you can: your attitudes, motives, choices, and faithfulness.

5. **Time allows us to see with new and hopefully more mature eyes.**
   - » Be patient and wait upon the Lord's guidance.

6. **Serve someone else in greater need than yourself.**
   - » This helps the person and grows you.

7. **Be thankful in everything.**
   - » This is both a prayer and a step of faith at the same time.

You are now challenged to go make a difference in the world. You have the light, hope, and power of Christ living in and through you to impact a world that is in desperate need of the reality of Christ. You are equipped to see, think, choose, act, and live from a new vantage point and to enter a path of possibility, knowing that "all things are possible with God." Keep in mind that we are living an eternal life in the moment and for just a moment here on earth. How we live that life will impact eternity in our lives and the lives around us.

You have the power of perspective—now go change the world!

ABOUT THE AUTHOR

Bruce R. Witt is President of Leadership Revolution Inc., a non-profit organization dedicated to developing and multiplying servant leaders who live as Christ and mobilize others to reach their world. He began his career in marketing for Shell Oil Company in the solid plastics area. He was led to join the Christian Business Men's Committee where he directed the U.S. field operations and authored several key curriculum for the ministry, including the Operation Timothy spiritual development series and the Lighthouse evangelism curriculum.

In 2008, after seeing the tremendous need for leaders to understand and practice Christ as the Leader in their entire life, Bruce was led to form Leadership Revolution in order to establish a process that would help leaders truly allow Christ to be their leader.

Bruce has written curriculum and training resources and he regularly travels throughout the United States and the globe conducting workshops, conferences and train the trainer sessions to spread the vision and empower others to follow Christ as their leader. Along with partner organizations and churches, Bruce has trained thousands of leaders and trained hundreds of trainers who can also train others.

Bruce has been married to his wife Dana for 40 years and they have two grown sons—Robert, married to Allison, and Andrew, married to Amy, who have three sons: Brooks, Harrison, and Cooper.

THE BROADER PLAN FOR YOUR LEADERSHIP DEVELOPMENT

What are the greatest challenges that you face as a leader? In this in-depth, foundational book, *There is One Leader and You Are...Not it!*, Bruce Witt shares the seven foundational principles that Jesus Christ, the One Leader, established to eternally impact the world around us.

ISBN 978-0-9965714-1-8
228 pages, Softcover

Everyone faces mountains and valleys in life—that is a fact. The question is how do we experience victory in them? We can have triumph in Christ in every circumstance! Is this too good to be true? Is it some overly positive mental attitude, or can it be a reality? This is a book about living with hope in life's difficulties and progressing while doing well.

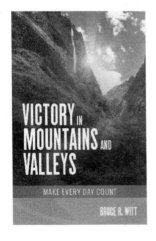

ISBN 978-0-9965714-9-4
164 pages, Softcover

Order from Amazon.com or www.LeadershipRevolution.us